Max Weber on Universities

MAX WEBER
On Universities

*The Power of the State
and the Dignity
of the Academic Calling
in Imperial Germany*

*Translated, Edited
and with an Introductory Note by*
Edward Shils

The University of Chicago Press
Chicago and London

The University of Chicago Press, Chicago 60637
The University of Chicago Press, Ltd., London
Reprinted from *Minerva,* vol. 11, no. 4 (October 1973)
© 1973 *Minerva.* All rights reserved
Published 1974
Printed in Great Britain
International Standard Book Number: 0-226-87726-4
Library of Congress Catalog Card Number: 73-94103

CONTENTS

Introductory Note 1

I. The Bernhard Affair 4

II. A Supplementary Note on the "Bernhard Affair" 8

III. The "Bernhard Affair" and Professor Delbruck 9

IV. The Alleged "Academic Freedom" of the German Universities 14

V. The Academic Freedom of the Universities 18

VI. American and German Universities 23

A Reply to Max Weber 30

VII. Max Weber on the "Althoff System" 31

A Second Reply to Max Weber 34

VIII. Max Weber and the Althoff System 34

IX. The Schools of Economics 36

X. Remarks Supplementing the Talks at Dresden 39

XI. The "Althoff System" Once Again 43

XII. A Catholic University in Salzburg 46

XIII. The Meaning of "Ethical Neutrality" in Sociology and Economics 47

XIV. Science as a Vocation 54

The Power of the State and the Dignity of the Academic Calling in Imperial Germany

THE WRITINGS OF MAX WEBER
ON UNIVERSITY PROBLEMS

INTRODUCTORY NOTE

MAX WEBER was born in 1864 and died in 1920. At the beginning of his career he worked in ancient and medieval economic and legal history. He began his academic career as *Privatdozent* at the University of Berlin where he taught law. In 1893 he became professor of economics at the University of Freiburg and in 1896 was called to Heidelberg again as professor of economics in succession to Karl Knies. He had to renounce teaching on grounds of ill-health in 1903 and did not resume again until 1918. In spite of his illness, he was able to accomplish a prodigious amount of research in the history of Western and Asian religions, and in social, economic and legal history, as well as a large investigation into the industrial working class. He also edited the *Archiv für Sozialwissenschaft und Sozialpolitik*, which from his assumption of editorship in 1904 until its closure in 1933 was one of the leading social science periodicals in the world. In addition to this he wrote a great deal about contemporary politics and during the First World War he began to take a more active part in politics. He was, although a nationalist, a severe critic of the emperor and of programmes of territorial annexation.

During the period of his retirement from teaching he continued to live in Heidelberg and played a central part in the extraordinarily rich intellectual life there. It was also during the period of his retirement from teaching that he wrote most of the works which were posthumously published as *Gesammelte Aufsätze zur Religionssoziologie*, 2nd edn., 3 vols., (Tübingen: J. C. B. Mohr [Paul Siebeck], 1922–23); *Gesammelte Aufsätze zur Wissenschaftslehre* (Tübingen: J. C. B. Mohr [Paul Siebeck], 1922); *Wirtschaft und Gesellschaft*, 2 vols., (Tübingen: J. C. B. Mohr [Paul Siebeck], 1922); *Gesammelte Aufsätze zur Soziologie und Sozialpolitik* (Tübingen: J. C. B. Mohr [Paul Siebeck], 1924) and *Gesammelte Aufsätze zur Sozial- und Wirtschaftsgeschichte* (Tübingen: J. C. B. Mohr [Paul Siebeck], 1924). On these rest his reputation as one of the very greatest figures in the history of the social sciences. His range of erudition was universal, his analytical penetration and scope were equal to his erudition. Although his research dealt with ancient Israel, China, India, Rome and the Reformation, his pervasive concern was with the character, origin and fate of modern Western society. He was a liberal who regarded Bismarck—whom he also admired for his great political talent and achievements—as the source of Germany's political incapacity. He thought that the long and artful ascendancy of Bismarck had had disastrous consequences for Germany because he had crushed the incipient civility which had existed and never permitted any new civility to grow up again. Lacking a sense of civil self-esteem and a sense of responsibility for their own actions, the German people showed no inclination or capacity to maintain their independence in the face of political leaders of charismatic genius and a powerful bureaucracy. When he contemplated the German universities of his own time, Max Weber saw a similar phenomenon. He thought that the members of the academic profession in Germany were losing the sense of the dignity of their academic role. As in the political sphere, they were being manipulated by a powerful figure, Friedrich Althoff, who held all the strings in his hand, who dazzled, outwitted, seduced and corrupted the academic profession. Weber thought that German university professors deceived themselves about the narrow constraints within which their academic freedom existed, and that they had no insight into the enfeebling influence which their readiness to bow before the prestige and power of the imperial monarchy and its political and administrative agents was having on their traditions.

Max Weber made no predictions about the conduct of German professors in the period of adversity which followed his death. Preoccupied as he was in the last years of his life with the completion of his great works—which were left incomplete—with the public disorder of German life after the defeat, and with his own re-commenced teaching activities (1918 in Vienna and 1919 in Munich), he wrote nothing more on the themes of his earlier journalistic publications on the universities and the state. Nevertheless the capitulation of so many German academic figures to the Nazi regime may be plausibly interpreted as evidence of the correctness of Max Weber's diagnosis regarding the complaisance of the German academic profession in its eager subservience to the authority of the state and the erosion of its moral rectitude.

Most of Weber's writings on the problems of the German university in the face of political and bureaucratic authority were published in the *Frankfurter Zeitung*. These and his four other short occasional articles have never been reprinted or collected [1] and none of them has ever been translated. They have been assembled and translated for publication in *Minerva,* not just because they are rare minor works of one of the great intellects of modern times but rather because they state, albeit in a particular context and in controversial form, certain fundamental principles of the liberal conception of university autonomy and academic freedom. Max Weber's principles embodied, around two thirds of a century ago, in these brief polemic articles, merit the attention and reflection of *Minerva's* readers.

In addition to these more occasional polemics, Max Weber dealt with university problems in several of his other writings. In 1917 he published a long paper on the relationship between evaluations or judgements of value and empirical or factual knowledge. It was the outcome of his effort over many years to make economists aware that their recommendations for particular policies did not arise solely from their economic-scientific studies but were based on certain ethical and political postulates which he wished them to acknowledge. In the introductory part of this paper, he examined the question of whether university teachers of the social sciences should present their own ethical and political evaluations in the course of their teaching, and the conditions and forms in which it would be legitimate for them to do so. I have reproduced the pertinent section of this paper because it expresses Max Weber's view that the university teacher must, if he wishes to express his views about authority and the policies it should follow, take the responsibility for doing so on himself and not allow it to appear that it is unquestionably " given " by the " facts " and hence lies outside his own moral responsibility.

In 1919 he delivered a lecture to an association of students of the

---

[1] Professor Johannes Winckelmann of the Max Weber Institute of Munich provided me with the otherwise unobtainable copies of the original texts.

University of Munich on "Science as a Vocation". This is one of the deepest and most moving confessions of faith in the value of science and scholarship coupled with a tragic awareness of their limits. The first part of this talk deals with the risks of the academic career and it leads into the discussion of the grounds of the pursuit of knowledge. I have reproduced these pages of *Wissenschaft als Beruf* in this section of *Minerva* because it complements the argument, put forward in his journalistic writings, that an individual sense of responsibility and corporate self-respect are the preconditions of fruitful intellectual accomplishment and the university's discovery and performance of its proper function in society.

E. S.

I

THE BERNHARD AFFAIR [2]

THE articles in the press about the much discussed " Bernhard affair " by no means exhaust its interest. The scandal lies in the fact that the government—or more precisely the minister on his personal initiative—has imposed a professor on the largest university in Germany and that the scholars in the fields affected, who are to be counted among the most respected men of learning in Germany, first learned of the situation from the press or through the visits of their new colleague. But certain other aspects are perhaps even more significant. First is the behaviour of the person who was so suddenly promoted. At a time when the author of these lines was as young as Herr Bernhard is now, one of the most elementary requirements of academic decency was that anyone who was invited by a ministry to take up a professorship made certain, above all else and before he decided, that he enjoyed the intellectual confidence of the faculty—or at least of the most outstanding colleagues in his own field, whose cooperation he would need. He would have done this regardless of whether he was apprehensive that as a result there would be difficulties in attaining the post, even if these were only of a moral nature. There have been persons who, because the " market situation " was " favourable " to them, infringed on those self-evident rules in order to " get ahead " academically. Such persons were subjected to the same judgement and treated by their colleagues in the same way as they treated those others who, for purposes of professional advancement, took the chance of obtaining an ecclesiastically or politically imposed professorship.

Once we take note of the fact that Herr Bernhard did not find it necessary to pay any attention to these rules, we need say nothing more about him personally. Of more general significance, however, is the fact that this type of attitude is obviously becoming more common among some sectors of the new generation of academics. It is also of general importance that the Prussian government is breeding this type of " operator "—as such an individual is called in academic usage. There

[2] " Der Fall Bernhard ", *Frankfurter Zeitung*, 18 June, 1908 (unsigned).
Ludwig Bernhard who was born in 1875, was appointed to a full professorship of economics at the University of Berlin in 1908 on the initiative of Friedrich Althoff, head of the department of university affairs in the Prussian Ministry of Education. The appointment was made without as much as consultation with the appropriate faculty of the university. By a convention which had become well established in the course of the nineteenth century, professorial appointments in German universities were made on the proposal of a short list of acceptable nominees to the minister with whom the official power of appointment lay and who then decided which candidate to appoint. Although the minister was not bound to confine his choice to candidates on the list, he usually did so.
Bernhard had taught at the academy at Posen and then at the Universities of Greifswald and Kiel for a short period before his elevation to the professorship at Berlin. In 1907 he published *Die Polenfrage* in which he dealt with the Polish immigration into East Prussia. This immigration was associated with the immigrants' employment as seasonal agricultural labourers on the large landed estates, and with the corresponding decline of German tenant farmers and agricultural labour. In the early 1890s, Max Weber had conducted a large-scale enquiry into the situation of the East Elban agricultural workers on behalf of the Verein für Sozialpolitik. [Editor.]

are today professorial chairs which are regularly used to provide for these types.

As regards the University of Berlin itself, appointment to a professorship there is naturally deemed a financially profitable affair. However, the time when it was regarded as a great scientific or scholarly distinction has passed. Certainly we are happy to see that even today in Berlin in many fields there are men who are leading figures of science and scholarship and who are at the same time men of absolutely independent character. But the number of compliant mediocrities who are much sought after because of their compliancy is growing, apparently more rapidly there than elsewhere. Now persons of Herr Bernhard's type come along—persons for whom, from the government's point of view, appointment to the university is essentially an act of patronage conferring financial and social advantages.

It is to a certain extent fortunate for the provincial universities that, as a result of this situation, a much larger number of outstanding scholars and scientists remain in the provinces than would be the case if, in appointments to professorial posts in Berlin, only scientific and scholarly criteria were applied. Naturally these matters must be judged differently from the standpoint of the University of Berlin. A partly successful and partly unsuccessful effort is being made in a number of faculties of the University of Berlin, to limit the number of professorships, while simultaneously the number of students is increasing; at the same time, one faculty has enacted a rule to limit the habilitation of teachers from other universities and has attempted to use this restriction of its own making as a means of preventing an admittedly outstanding scholar from becoming a *Privatdozent;* this has happened against the vote of the qualified experts.[3] It is a peculiar irony that the very university in which such things have happened is now willing to allow its professorships to be used for purposes of patronage, whenever a ministry thinks it needs to have some politically desirable research undertaken by a competent young man.[4]

---

[3] Max Weber presumably referred to Werner Sombart's failure to obtain the right of habilitation at the University of Berlin while he was teaching at Breslau.

It had been the almost universal procedure in Germany for those who sought to pursue an academic career—and ultimately to attain a professorship—to habilitate. Habilitation entailed the submission of a monograph containing the results of original research some years after having received a doctoral degree; this monograph was required to be considerably more substantial than the doctoral dissertation. In addition to this, the candidate delivered a public lecture before the faculty and was then nominally examined by them. He was then admitted to the status of *Privatdozent.* He received no salary; he received only the capitation fees of those students who attended his lectures. At the same time, he was free to lecture on whatever subject he chose within his general field of competence. The *Privatdozent,* unlike the professor, was not a government official. Having none of the privileges he was also free of the obligations imposed by membership in the civil service. His appointment was entirely an internal university affair; the government of the state had no legal jurisdiction there. (The *lex Arons* was a departure from this arrangement. See *infra,* pp. 15–16). Professors, particularly full (or " ordinary ") professors were nearly always chosen from the reservoir of *Privatdozenten.* See Busch, Alexander, " The Vicissitudes of the *Privatdozent*: Breakdown and Adaptation in the Recruitment of the German University Teacher ", *Minerva,* I, 3 (Spring 1963), pp. 319–341 ; a fuller account may be found in the same author's *Die Geschichte des Privatdozenten: Eine soziologische Studie zur grossbetrieblichen Entwicklung der deutschen Universitäten* (Stuttgart: Ferdinand Enke Verlag, 1959). [Editor.]

[4] Whether this is the decisive factor in the particular case under consideration need not be settled here. Persons who have an intimate acquaintance with the conditions prevailing

All concessions which the faculties make to non-intellectual considerations, and particularly all deviations from the fundamental principle of appointing as many intellectually outstanding persons as possible, take their revenge in the ultimate weakening of the moral authority of the faculties. Naturally, the results of this are not only seen in cases like the one with which we are now confronted. Herr Bernhard, whatever his scholarly immaturity, has written a solid book which gave evidence of some distinctiveness of method; it was—to me at least—an impressive piece of work. But everyone knows that, for example, in economics, there were at least two other persons at the door of the faculty who had " merits ' of diverse sorts; in the case of one of them, these extended as far back as the " Stumm epoch ".[5] Sooner or later the course of events would certainly have had to turn in their favour.

It appears quite improbable that men like Adolf Wagner and Schmoller will have successors who are at once outstanding in character and scientifically distinguished. It is similar in other Prussian universities. They no longer have to deal with the powerful figure of Herr Althoff who, despite all that was problematic about his " system ", still possessed a certain grandeur. Rather their fate is now in the custody of personally friendly but frightfully inferior and petty " operators "; it is in the hands of persons whose influence will for the foreseeable future create a favourable " market " for the ascent of compliant academic " operators " in accordance with the law by which, as experience shows, one mediocrity in a faculty brings others in his train. In all such future " affairs ", as is the case in the present one, the Berlin faculties particularly, will only have the freedom to choose the form by which they will put a good face on improper action. The members of that university will be incapable of offering any resistance to public opinion or to the government because of the weakening of their moral authority, which they have themselves helped to bring about. And as a result of this, in the future an increasing proportion of their colleagues will act no differently.

It is obviously to be recognised that in the University of Berlin, as elsewhere, there are not a few men of strong character who continue the proud tradition of academic solidarity and independence *vis-à-vis* the higher authorities. But everyone knows that this group is not increasing. The door to the Ministry of Education is unfortunately much too near the Berlin professors for such a thing to happen. There has been an

---

in the official apparatus of the Ostmark could become rather inconvenient outside the Prussian sphere of power.

(The " official apparatus of the Ostmark " to which Weber referred in the foregoing paragraph, was a body which, by the use of government funds, was intended to settle German farmers in the Ostmark and to reverse the process of the replacement of the German cultivators by the seasonal Polish labour force. This organisation was much criticised and Professor Bernhard, in consequence of his studies for *Die Polenfrage*, could be assumed to know about occurrences within the organisation which high officials would wish to keep from reaching the public. Since, as a professor in a Prussian university and hence as a civil servant, he was bound by the disciplinary regulations of the civil service and dependent on the goodwill of the Prussian Ministry of Education, Professor Bernhard might be expected to remain silent as long as he remained within the borders of Prussia. [Editor.])

[5] Weber here refers to the period towards the end of the nineteenth century when Freiherr von Stumm, a wealthy, very conservative and illiberal industrialist, exercised much influence on the government. [Editor.]

increasing tendency towards the unsatisfactory situation in which Prussian " provincial professors " address requests and complaints to their actually or allegedly influential Berlin colleagues in the hope that the latter will intercede for them in " higher circles ". This exercise of power through personal relations with the Ministry—which has been developed in practically every field in more or less explicit form—has without doubt often been used by certain eminent Berlin scholars of strong character for the advancement of their subjects. But we must make the qualification that even where there is an honourable striving for objectivity in the assessment of intellectual merit, there is a danger of personal preferences and interests coming into play when one person controls so much patronage.

Today, however, conditions are beginning to change fundamentally. As the " Bernhard affair " has so strikingly shown, influence which rests on such personal relations, even when it is exercised by outstanding scholars at a time when " practical " considerations are becoming increasingly decisive, can turn out to be only a precarious pseudo-power. Not only do the various personal influences cancel each other out—it appears that in the present affair the conduct of a well-known theologian in the treatment of the appropriate experts was not quite disinterested—but, when persons of weaker character are involved, the government acquires a very definitely effective means of exploiting their vanity for its own purposes. The more Berlin University is made up of " operators ", the more likely it is that things will develop in such a way that the government will be forthcoming in all small matters towards those professors with whom, in its own interest, it maintains continuous " personal relations ", *e.g.*, it will take into account their testimonials for their protégés and the like—and thereby it will satisfy them. As a result, the patronage of the Berlin professors on behalf of the " provincial professors " will become a real even though unofficial institution. But at the same time, for this very reason, in those important matters in which the voice of the expert scholar as such and the authority of the faculty as such should be decisive, neither of them will in fact amount to anything. Whoever is accustomed to acting as a patron through using his personal connections for his personal protégés, renounces the moral weight which should be attributed to his opinion as an expert and as one who exercises power officially.

The development of the Berlin professorial corps in the direction just described does not appear susceptible to being stopped. This is a severe danger to the academic profession's sense of corporate solidarity. We still remember the passionate rebuke with which certain Berlin circles responded to the attempt to institute discussions by university teachers on the common concerns of all universities.[6] Even without such amiable counsel, no one can doubt that the sphere of influence of a trans-local university organisation, regardless of its basis, has by its very nature certain limits. Still, apart from discussing the important problems of university teaching, an organisation of university teachers with intelligent leadership could reawaken the sense of corporate pride of the next academic generation to offset the " practical point of view ", and it could thereby contribute to

---

[6] Weber here seems to be referring to the refusal of the Berlin professors to participate in the Deutschen Hochschullehrertag. See, *infra*, p. 10. [Editor.]

the gradual re-establishment of the diminishing moral weight of the universities. No one can really doubt this. The "Bernhard affair" has shown that both of these tasks are urgently necessary for Prussia. I will not discuss on this occasion the frequently embittering way in which the Prussian system and the influence of certain Berlin circles have recently begun to extend their powers beyond the borders of Prussia.

Finally, more general reflections on the future must reveal how pernicious is the growth of the "practical point of view" and the success of the professorial "guilds" with their patronage. The atmosphere and interests of political life are influencing governmental policy with regard to the universities. Such events as the "Bernhard affair", and situations of which this "affair" is a symptom, are bound to diminish gravely the respect with which university teachers are held by the student body. Whether this is permanently to the advantage of government, I leave it for the government to decide. May, in any case, events in the Austrian universities be a warning to their German sisters not to allow the moral credit which they still possess before public opinion and among their students to be destroyed—and not to destroy it by their own misdeeds.

II

A SUPPLEMENTARY NOTE ON THE "BERNHARD AFFAIR" [7]

THE author of the article (18 June, 1908) on the "Bernhard affair" writes that Professor Harnack [8] has informed him in the most categorical manner that he was just as surprised as everyone else by the appointment of Herr Bernhard, and that Professor Harnack has unequivocally declared that his judgement of the procedure is no different from theirs. To this should be added: (1) the view—which also was accepted in those circles which are most closely associated with and the best informed about the affair—to the effect that Professor Bernhard sought the advice at least of those who were closest to him, does an injustice on the one side to Professor Harnack, and, on the other, puts Professor Bernhard in too favourable a light; (2) the Minister did not seek the advice of any academic person although it has been untruthfully asserted that this was done. The ministerial declaration that there was no time to do so makes as grotesque

[7] Unsigned and untitled article, *Frankfurter Zeitung*, 24 June, 1908.
[8] The "well-known theologian" referred to in the "Bernhard affair" (*supra*, p. 7), was undoubtedly Professor Adolf Harnack (1851–1930) who was professor of church history at the University of Berlin from 1889 to 1921. From 1905 to 1921, he was also director of the Prussian Staatsbibliothek and from 1910 he was president of the Kaiser-Wilhelm-Gesellschaft (the predecessor of the present Max-Planck-Gesellschaft). He was the author of *Lehrbuch der Dogmengeschichte*, 1886–89 (translated into English as *History of Dogma*, 7 volumes [London: Williams and Norgate, 1894–99]), *Die Mission and Ausbreitung des Christentums in den ersten drei Jahrhunderte* (translated into English as *The Mission and Expansion of Christianity in its First Three Centuries*, 2nd edition, 2 volumes [London: Williams and Norgate, 1908]) and numerous other scholarly works. As a theologian, he was regarded as a liberal; he emphasised the claims of human brotherhood at the expense of the strictly doctrinal side of Christianity. In politics he was a moderate nationalist during the First World War, and during the last decade of his life he was one of minority of eminent German professors who supported the Weimar Republic. [Editor.]

an impression in the age of the telephone and the motor car as does the statement which Professor Bernhard presented to the Berlin faculty after a precedent had been created and the damage had been done.

With this the case is closed.

III

THE " BERNHARD AFFAIR " AND PROFESSOR DELBRÜCK [9]

AN acquaintance has sent me a copy of the *Preussische Jahrbücher* for July and I should like to make the following observations concerning Professor Delbrück who deals there with, among other matters, my article on the " Bernhard affair " in the *Frankfurter Zeitung* of 18 June, 1908.

First of all, despite the definiteness with which the opinion was accepted—without contradiction, in the press and in Berlin academic circles, and not just in individual cases—that Professor Harnack shared in the responsibility for the conduct of his close associate, Professor Bernhard, I had already taken account of the fact that this opinion was put forward in a form which could not be wholly relied on. I considered Professor Harnack's appeal

[9] " Der ' Fall Bernhard ' und Professor Delbrück ", *Frankfurter Zeitung*, 10 July, 1908.

Hans Delbrück was born in 1848 and died in 1929. He was editor of the *Preussische Jahrbucher* from 1883 to 1923, and professor of history at the University of Berlin from 1885 to 1921. He took an active part in politics as a Free Conservative Party member of the Reichstag and of the Prussian Diet. His main scholarly work was *Geschichte der Kriegskunst im Rahmen der politischen Geschichte*, 5 volumes (Berlin: George Stilke, 1900–1927). He was of a polemical disposition and often criticised particular governmental policies although he was deeply attached to the throne and the bureaucracy.

Delbrück's article to which Max Weber referred was entitled " Akademische Wirren " (" Academic Muddle "). It appeared in *Preussische Jarhbücher*, CXXXIII, 1 (July 1908), pp. 196–181, in the section devoted to editorial comment. In this article, Delbrück took the view that there were no grounds for criticising the mode of appointment followed in the Bernhard case. Although he asserted that as a member of the Berlin faculty and hence officially involved in the matter he could not express himself freely, he went on nonetheless to say that the formal rights of the faculty in matters of appointment were slight. The minister was not confined to recommendations made by the faculty, and in appointments to new chairs and to associate professorships, there was not even a statutory right of recommendation. Delbrück said that the fact that recommendations made by the faculty even for associate (*ausserordentliche*) professorships were generally accepted by the minister was nothing more than a convention. In so far as the minister understood what science and scholarship were, he was likely to exercise his power in consultation with the faculties and to accept their recommendations unless he had special reasons for not doing so. The well-being of the Prussian universities rested on good understanding between the government and the universities. All the more reason then for the avoidance of a public cleavage between the minister and the faculties. (Although Delbrück's statements seemed factually correct and although he showed much courage in opposing extreme forms of nationalism, in this instance, conciliatoriness towards Althoff illustrated exactly the attitude which Max Weber censured.)

Delbrück went on to criticise Professor Biermer of Giessen University for suggesting that Bernhard's appointment was the result of an intrigue by the " *Hakatists* ", *i.e.*, the members of the Ostmark organisation, and pointed out that Bernhard had been critical of the " *Hakatists* " in showing that the policy followed in East Prussia for two decades had failed. This indeed showed, according to Delbrück, that the Prussian government had manifested great freedom from prejudice in appointing one who was critical of its policies.

Delbrück then turned his attention more directly to Max Weber, whom he did not name but referred to repeatedly as " a South German professor ". He said that the latter wrote " all sorts of gossip of the most foolish sort ". He referred to Sombart also not by name, but as a " close friend of the South German anonym ". In justification of the denial of Sombart's application for habilitation, Delbrück said that many *Privatdozenten* from other

to me to " know " that he was " entirely astonished " by the affair, and that
he was not so " naïve " and " simple-minded " as " to be made responsible
for such a mode of procedure ": (1) as obviously not addressed to me in
my private capacity; (2) as a categorical denial of the opinion in question;
and (3) as an entirely unequivocal judgement on the affair. Accordingly, I
felt obliged to communicate his view to the *Frankfurter Zeitung.*[10]

How I could have acted differently is as inconceivable to me as it is to
anyone else. In Professor Harnack's subsequent letter dealing with the
Bernhard affair, there was not the slightest trace of an indication that he
thought he had been misunderstood in any way by this disclosure of his
views. When Delbrück now gives the impression, because it fits in with
his article, that Professor Harnack would have preferred that his attitude
had been withheld from the public eye, and when he says that I incorrectly
re-stated " the essential point " of Professor Harnack's views, he attributes
an equivocation to Professor Harnack which—in view of the letter which

universities wished to be habilitated again in Berlin in order to take advantage of the larger
audiences in Berlin, the University of Berlin being by far the largest in Germany; even
professors from provincal universities sometimes gave up their professorships to become
Privatdozenten in Berlin, where their audience might exceed that which they attracted as
full professors in the provinces. This was unsatisfactory, according to Delbrück, because
it placed the university faculties in the embarrassing situation of examining persons who
were already of acknowledged standing, and because it might therefore result in the
University of Berlin passing judgement by implication on the standards of other universities.
More serious however was the threat which such incursions of outside scholars brought to
the " real *Privatdozenten* "—it would take away their " air and light " to an " intolerable
extent ". There was, for example, a shortage of lecture rooms in the philosophical faculty.
Hence it had been decided to admit professors of other universities to habilitation only
when there was a demonstrated need " for their services ". No exception could be made
even for outstandingly talented scholars. " It seems to me to be very difficult to object to
such a regulation. What can we say when a South German professor pours a veritable
flood of abuse over the Berlin faculty because it applied its regulations a few years ago
to one of his friends? What would others have said if an exception had been made for
this friend?" Delbrück also made insulting insinuations that Max Weber had acted
improperly regarding Harnack.
    Delbrück acknowledged that there was sometimes a danger of uniformity of views in
German universities but said that it was not great because of the large number of separate
universities and separate state systems and the competition among them. In reply to the
charge that Schmoller would not tolerate any current of economics other than his own,
not only in Berlin but in Prussia as well, he cited the *Festschrift* presented to his " highly
esteemed and dear colleague ", Schmoller, on the occasion of his 70th birthday. Schmoller
" knew how to discover and cherish what was good in Junkers and agrarians and in social
democrats as well ". Delbrück cites the heterogeneity of the membership of the Verein für
Sozialpolitik which was Schmoller's creation. Thus it was untrue that Schmoller allowed
no other kind of economics than his own to emerge. The list of teachers of economics
at the University of Berlin showed clearly the falsehood of this assertion. Delbrück listed
a series of names, to some of which he added those qualifications which appeared to support his contention of diversity: among these were to be found " von Halle (privy counsellor of the Admiralty), Simmel (sociology), Jastrow (director of the Berlin School of
Economics), Zöpfle (colonies), . . . Dade (recently agrarian-conservative candidate for the
Reichstag ".
    In this same article, Delbrück delivered himself of a series of very disparaging observa-
tions concerning the recently formed Deutsche Hochschullehrertag, to which Max Weber
had referred towards the end of his first article. Delbrück had in fact already written an
extended, ill-argued and very derogatory polemic against this organisation in the preceding
year (" Eine Professorengewerkschaft ", *Preussische Jahrbücher*, CXXXIV, 1 (July 1907),
pp. 129–142.) For the origins of the Deutsche Hochschullehrertag, see Brentano, Lujo,
" Die Kampf um die Unabhängigkeit der Universitäten " in *Mein Leben im Kampf um die
soziale Entwicklung Deutschlands* (Jena: Eugen Diederichs Verlag, 1931), pp. 281–288.
[Editor].
    10 Published on 24 June, 1908. (Article II above. [Editor.])

I have in my possession—is ridiculous. No respectable person, however great his difference of views, would regard Professor Harnack as capable of such an equivocation.

This example of completely thoughtless prattle, which cites not a single incorrect statement, a single insulting or even a merely passionate word, is sufficient to evaluate Delbrück's claim that my article "abounds in incorrect assertions", pours a "flood of insult" over the Berlin faculty, and is made up of "dull gossip". My critic knows very well that even where I expressed myself in very general terms—as for example when I wrote of the "Ostmark-apparatus" or about "patronage"— I said nothing for which I would be unable to provide adequate instances if I were absolutely forced to it. His courage in producing these rhetorical flowers rests on his justified confidence that I would not find it fitting to present examples in which persons are identified by name.

As regards Professor Bernhard personally, I am pleased to state that I have been assured by those who are friendly to him that his motives have been too unfavourably assessed. Unfortunately, they have done this without producing any tangible evidence which could provide me with an explanation, or with the very agreeable obligation of saying that only appearances have been against him. His subsequent conduct is certainly not sufficient for this purpose. It is important to come out with clean hands from the office of the Ministry of Culture—I know from my own experience that this has by no means been easy in Prussia since Althoff established his own procedural style—but it is more important than what is done subsequently in public and under the pressure of publicity. Professor Bernhard, both before and since, bears the responsibility for a situation which has seriously damaged the position of the academic profession in Prussia, which had already been very insecure, quite apart from this affair. The paltry and malicious pettiness of the "most influential" circles is amply shown by the fact that, in the celebrations in honour of the man who certainly contributed more than anyone else alive to the glorification of the Prussian monarchy, the Prussian Ministry of Culture, out of pure spite, was not represented.

At the end of his article, Professor Delbrück rushes passionately to defend his "highly esteemed and dear colleague", Professor Schmoller, from attacks—whose?—on his impartiality. In order to show what diverse tendencies are represented in our own discipline in Berlin, we are presented with a list of teachers there, to which are added such descriptions as "privy counsellor of the Admiralty", "sociologist", "statistician", "agrarian candidate for the Reichstag", etc. It is certainly reassuring that, alongside the "sociologist's outlook", the "outlooks" of the "privy counsellor of the Admiralty", of the "agrarians", and of the "statisticians" are represented. We have only to observe about this logically remarkable classification, that the names of scholars who work or worked in very different fields, such as philosophy and history, have been misappropriated on behalf of the "social sciences" and—this is the important point—that their degrading treatment at the hands of the decisive authorities in Berlin has for many years remained the very opposite

of a mark of honour for the entire German university system.[11]   To deal
with this would not have fitted into Delbrück's article.

With these remarks I begin to approach that point which Delbrück
treats most broadly and in a manner which unfortunately compels me,
against my will, to speak " personally ".   I have indicated a few cases in
which the conduct of those in power was unnecessary and injurious to the
authority of the faculties.   If it were to serve some practical purpose, I
would develop this further.   Professor Delbrück seizes on the case of the
rejection of Professor Sombart's [12] application for habilitation in Berlin.
Against whatever he adduces in the way of " facts ", it is sufficient to state
what has repeatedly been pointed out: the experts, Adolf Wagner and
Schmoller, who are undoubtedly more competent on the problems of
" needs " than Delbrück, were despite the excessively widely proclaimed
" decision " of the faculty, strongly in favour of Sombart's admission.   This
should be sufficient for us.   All the more so—and Delbrück too could know
about this—since all sorts of very miserable personal gossip, which had to
be countered first by outsiders, was brought to bear in the argument against
admission.   As the circumstances showed, there was no question of any
strictly scholarly or formal difficulties; considerations of personality
outweighed all others.

It is correct that certain personal experiences did play a part in
compelling my attention to this matter.   Not long before, it had been
suggested to me privately but by very important groups in the Berlin
faculty that I should do formally what Professor Sombart was soon to be
prevented from doing.   It was suggested to me by what procedure a need
could be found for my admission, which was not forthcoming for Professor
Sombart's.   I think of Delbrück's remarks about the threat of such
habilitation to the " light and air " of the " real *Privatdozenten* ".   I have
for many years been unable on grounds of health to carry out the teaching
duties for which I am qualified—that is why at the time I rejected the
suggestion.   Consequently I would not have been in the position in which
Professor Sombart probably was, to take away their " light and air " from
our Berlin colleagues, as Delbrück very tastefully calls it, or, in plain
German, lecture audiences and lecture fees.   Hence, my qualifications for
appointment at the University of Berlin would have been superior, according to the principles now enunciated explicitly and publicly by Delbrück.

[11] Weber presumably referred to the case of the eminent philosopher and sociologist,
George Simmel, who, despite his widely acknowledged achievements, was never appointed
to a full professorship at Berlin because he was of Jewish origin. [Editor].

[12] Werner Sombart was born in 1863 and died in 1941. He was extraordinary professor
of economics at the University of Breslau from 1890 until 1906 when he became a full
professor at the Berlin School of Economics. He became full professor at the University
of Berlin only in 1918.   In his early years he was in sympathy with Marxian socialism,
wrote favourably on the third volume of *Das Kapital* and entered into correspondence
with Friedrich Engels who was favourably inclined towards him. His socialist and Marxist
sympathies became attenuated by the end of the century but the disapproval of him because
of his earlier views persisted. He was also something of a bohemian and aesthete in his
personal affairs and this too was apparently held against him. He entered into close contact with Max Weber and became associated with him in editing the *Archiv für Sozialwissenschaft und Sozialpolitik.* He published a series of important works on German
economic history of the nineteenth century, the history of modern capitalism, the con-
tribution of the Jews to modern capitalism, luxury and capitalism, war and capitalism,
and the history of socialism and the labour movement in the 19th century. [Editor.]

Instead of taking satisfaction in that, my sense of propriety found such ideas abhorrent; this is something which I cannot alter. I think that the same is probably true of our colleagues in Berlin, who according to Delbrück are so much " in need of protection ". I think furthermore that invoking the " argument " of " light and air "—which should be regarded as belonging to those academic *pudenda* which I was inconsiderate enough to lay bare—does more to discredit universities than a dozen articles by me could do.

Enough of this. Delbrück puts before his public in all seriousness the contention that my matter-of-fact exposition in this newspaper on 18 June [1908] was impelled by personal motives. If this came from anyone else, I would treat it simply as infamous. But, unfortunately, the thing should not be taken so seriously, as far as he is concerned. Such expressions, and many others like them, have for a long time given his arguments a bad reputation; they are not conscious and deliberate indecencies towards his opponents as much as they are manifestations of a " coarseness " of sensibility which is a product of his journalistic activity. He is a dilettante in the field of journalism, unlike his great rival Maximilian Harden whom he hates so bitterly. He has acquired from the art of journalism something dilettantes always try to acquire nowadays, *i.e.*, its external routine. He is, God knows, not the great master of diplomacy he thinks himself to be but still, even as a politician, he is a clever man with a point of view, and not infrequently he has some interesting ideas, or at least some amusing paradoxes. But, at the same time, he lacks the sense of responsibility of the genuinely professional journalist. One should not therefore be disturbed by things which he does and for which a professional journalist would never be forgiven. At no time is he short-handed for a few phrases or arguments, whatever their significance, as long as they can be used in an article. Just because he is a dilettante, he thinks that in journalism, even of the " diplomatic " sort, this is how it always is, just as the peasant thinks that trade is always a swindle. I am convinced on the basis of my own experiences which cannot be interpreted otherwise, that this thoroughly naïve coarseness is the source of that absolutely complacent inability to understand the obligation to distinguish between personal considerations and the truthful analysis of facts.

A person who takes such an attitude naturally sees nothing wrong in lightly accusing an antagonist, who very seriously espouses a certain position, of wanting to do a favour for a " close friend " (or indeed to revenge himself on the faculty). In Delbrück's mind, this is not even a serious charge. The fact that he thinks in this manner, and that the practice of such a way of thinking is one of the traits which gives a certain liveliness to that type of journalism, also deprives it of any dignity; I certainly cannot take much pleasure in it. In any case, that is the way it is and " ethical judgements " are powerless in the face of such naïvety; one must, for better or for worse, grant it a sort of " fool's freedom ". Treitschke had an apt characterisation of it in his own time.

I should like to make one general observation in concluding this unwholesome discussion. Delbrück touches on what he calls the " professorial trade union ", which I cited as an illustration and from active participation in

which I have been hindered hitherto. It is of quite secondary importance
whether university teachers in the future come together in this or in some
other type of organisation. But if those who think like Delbrück are
successful for some time to come in preventing any such organised
expression of the " public opinion " of the academic profession—and I
regard it as by no means impossible that they will succeed in this effort,
at least for a while—then an inevitable consequence will be that individual
teachers in their isolation will be led to resort to using the press in order
to express themselves.

The serious press has hitherto, I think for very good reasons, been very
reserved in its treatment of academic matters. This is bound to change
fundamentally if present conditions persist. According to the "ideal"
contended for by Delbrück and many of his Berlin colleagues, the government should appoint outstanding individuals—apparently it will know
where to find them—and it may disregard duly constituted authorities and
organisations. If this "ideal", which has failed so miserably in the
" Bernhard affair " continues to be espoused in practice, one inevitable
consequence, among others, will be that the critical public discussion of
university matters will, whether it is desired or not, increasingly assume
the character of personal conflicts and of mutual denunciation. No one
really wants this. But such will be the unavoidable outcome of the views
which are represented by Delbrück as well as others, and as the foregoing
observations must unfortunately demonstrate, it will also be the outcome
of his own unprincipled conduct.

IV

THE ALLEGED " ACADEMIC FREEDOM " OF
THE GERMAN UNIVERSITIES [13]

THE second conference of German teachers in institutions of higher
education (Deutscher Hochschullehrertag) which is to take place in Jena
is to deal, among other questions, with the question of " academic freedom ". Of the " main themes " which Professor von Amira has published
in the supplement to the *Münchener Neusten Nachrichten*, it is evident
that in his eyes clericalism is the sole—or at least main—obstacle to
academic freedom.[14] This is understandable enough in view of the situation

[13] " Die sogenannte ' Lehrfreiheit ' an den deutschen Universitäten ", *Frankfurter Zeitung*,
20 September 1908.
[14] In 1901, Martin Spahn was appointed to a full professorship—the second on the
faculty—of medieval and modern history at the University of Strassburg. The appointment
was ordered by the government to be made according to criteria of religious adherence;
the first chair was to be reserved for Protestants, the second for Roman Catholics. The
faculty addressed the Kaiser in an effort to have the appointment rescinded. The Kaiser
disregarded the appeal; instead he confirmed the appointment by a telegram which said
that he was pleased " to be able to demonstrate to his Roman Catholic subjects that
acknowledged scholarly merit would always be employed by him for the benefit of the
fatherland ". Professor Lujo Brentano, who was then rector of the University of Munich,
after consultation with his colleagues, gained the support of the most famous classical
historian of the nineteenth century, Theodor Mommsen at Berlin, and a widespread
academic protest ensued on behalf of the " objectivity of research " (" *die Voraussetzungs-*

in Bavaria. It remains however for us to ask (1) whether academic freedom is really endangered only from this source, and (2) above all, whether today we really possess something which can reasonably be called "academic freedom", and if there is still something essential in this field which clericalism can infringe. At the jubilee celebration at the University of Jena, the rector, Professor Delbrück, spoke reassuringly in referring to a well known and large benefaction which had been given to the university under the express condition that academic freedom would be maintained; Professor Delbrück said that academic freedom in Jena was guaranteed by that provision. This distinguished scholar is either mistaken about the actual state of affairs, including that at the University of Jena, or he understands by "academic freedom" something essentially different from what many others understand by it—including, if I may say so, the benefactor himself if he were still alive. What the real situation is may be shown by an example of what has really happened.

Dr. Robert Michels,[15] who has meanwhile become known through a number of valuable works and who for many years lived as a private scholar in Marburg, decided to seek habilitation. Since in Prussia—as a result of the enforcement of the *lex Arons*—[16] there would be no chance

---

losigkeit der Wissenschaft "). See Brentano, Lujo, " Mein Kampf für die Freiheit der Wissenschaft ", *op. cit.*, pp. 217–226, and Rossmann, Kurt, *Wissenschaft, Ethik und Politik: Erörterung des Grundsatzes der Voraussetzungslosigkeit in der Forschung: Mit erstmaliger Veröffentlichung der Briefe Theodor Mommsens über den "Fall Spahn" und der Korrespondenz zu Mommsens öffentlicher Erklärung uber " Universitätsunterricht und Konfession" aus dem Nachlass Lujo Brentanos*, (Heidelberg: Lambert Schneider, 1949).

The Professor Delbrück to whom Max Weber referred in the text above was Berthold Delbrück (born 1842, died 1922); he became full professor of Sanskrit and comparative philology at the University of Jena in 1872 and remained at that university for the rest of his career. He made important contributions to the study of Indo-European, classical and Germanic philology. [Editor.]

15 Robert Michels was born in Cologne in 1876 of a German-French-Belgian family. He became a socialist as a young man and participated in the annual congresses of the Social Democratic Party in 1903, 1904 and 1905. He very early showed a sympathy with revolutionary syndicalism of the French style and his attack on the Social Democratic Party was directed primarily at the discrepancy between that party's revolutionary theory and rhetoric on the one side, and its moderation in practice and its bureaucratic structure on the other. He left the party in 1907. Having failed to gain admission to an academic career in Germany, he became a *libero docente* in Turin under the sponsorship of Achille Loria, at that time, a prominent economist of Marxian socialist sympathies. His subsequent academic career was made in Basel, Rome, Florence and Perugia. His book *Zur Soziologie des Parteiwesens: Untersuchungen über die oligarchischen Tendenzen des Gruppenlebens* (Leipzig: Kroner, 1911) translated as *Political Parties: A Sociological Study of the Oligarchical Tendencies of Modern Democracy* (London: Jarrold, 1916) has been for many years one of the classic works of the social sciences. Another book, *Il proletariato e la borghesia nel movimento socialista italiano: Saggio di scienza sociografico-politica* (Turino: Bocca, 1908) was a highly original investigation. It was these which Max Weber had in mind when he referred to Michels' accomplishments following his exclusion from German academic life. [Editor.]

16 Leo Arons (1860–1919) was *Privatdozent* in physics at the University of Berlin; he was also a member of the Social Democratic Party and a Jew. He had spoken in public meetings organised by his party. Charges were laid against him by the Ministry. The philosophical faculty of the University of Berlin constituted the disciplinary tribunal of the first instance; it found for Dr. Arons. It declared that his political views did not intrude into his teaching and that further, being a *Privatdozent* and hence not an official, his activities did not come under the jurisdiction of the Ministry. The faculty was not "able to discover any political danger to the state in the fact that a *Privatdozent* of physics was an active member of the Social Democratic Party", (Paulsen, Friedrich: *The German Universities and University Study* [New York: Charles Scribner & Sons, 1908], p. 251). The Ministry of Education was not satisfied and procured the enactment by the Reichstag of a law (*Gesetz über die Rechtsverhältnisse der Privatdozenten*, 17 June, 1898) which

for him as a member of the Social Democratic Party, he addressed himself
to Jena, relying on that provision mentioned by Professor Delbrück. He
inquired privately, in order to avoid a mis-step, whether his membership
in that party would stand in the way of his habilitation. The scholar of
whom he made this inquiry felt compelled to answer that, according to the
information available to him, it would be "quite impossible" in the
existing circumstances for his application for habilitation to pass the prescribed sequence of authorities from faculty to the senate and then to the
government. Nothing was said in the letter which conveyed this information—and there was naturally no obligation to say it—about the level at
which the obstacles would emerge. Nor was anything said about whether
the faculty would, if the occasion were to arise, protest as vigorously
against the exclusion of a political heretic from teaching as the faculty in
Berlin did under Schmoller's leadership, bearing in mind that the teaching
role in question was not that of a professor appointed by the state but
that of a teacher who, having no official appointment, was not subject to
state control. What is in any case clear is that the situation as far as the
candidate is concerned is the very opposite of "academic freedom"—as
has been acknowledged in Jena as well—and that these conditions contra-
dict, at least in spirit, the provisions of the aforementioned benefaction.

Even more characteristic than this occurrence itself was the sequence
of events which followed it. Dr. Michels, reluctant to receive further
rebuffs, was habilitated at the University of Turin, where he is now
officially charged with teaching duties and still belongs openly to the Social
Democratic Party; some of the most radical leaders of that party occupy,
on governmentally approved appointment, professorships in Italian
universities. It should be stated explicitly that the conditions of habilitation
in Italy are more subject to rigorous application of scientific and scholarly
criteria than is the case in Germany because there, in contrast with
Germany, the approving vote of the specialist of the particular university
is not normally the sole condition of admission. Where the local expert's
opinion is the decisive factor, this always brings with it the possibility
of favouring one's own pupils and friends and colleagues who share one's
own outlook. In Italy, the decision of the particular university is subject
to review by a national body which includes scholars from all over the
country—the rapporteur in Turin was Professor Achille Loria; the rapporteur in the central national body was a scholar of conservative political
views and the habilitation monograph dealt with Italian problems.

At last years' congress of teachers in institutions of higher education,
Professor Alfred Weber mentioned this case as an example of an infringement on academic freedom without citing the name of the university.
Professor Theodor Fisher of Marburg, obviously thinking that his university
was being referred to, replied that the person in question (Dr. Michels)
"could not, for quite different reasons, expect habilitation"; for this

brought *Privatdozenten* under governmental control in the expression of political opinion
by invoking a law of 1852 regarding the discipline of civil servants. On Althoff's conduct
in this matter see Paulsen, Friedrich, *An Autobiography* (New York: Columbia University
Press, 1938), pp. 363–365. Paulsen's account of his conversations with Althoff corresponds
completely with Max Weber's analysis of Althoff's conception of the relations of the
universities and the state. [Editor.]

reason " he shook the dust of his fatherland from his feet ". When in reading the proceedings I saw this remark which made no sense to me, I thought that he probably meant that the unrestrained candour with which Michels had criticised conditions in the ossified German Social Democratic Party might have annoyed that party. But I was mistaken. When Dr. Michels, with whom I had in the meantime become personally acquainted, learned of that statement during a visit to Heidelburg, he sought an explanation. He received a reply from Professor Fisher to the effect that the decisive reason was (1) " not just the fact of his social democratic beliefs but their public and exceptionally visible expression;" and (2) his family life: could Dr. Michels—who, lest we forget something " important ", is an " Aryan "—have even for a moment doubted that a man who would *not allow his children to be baptised* would be " impossible in any high ranking position "? The reply went on to say: " What a wonderful position you would have been able to obtain in Marburg where you were so well recommended and where *many influential persons* looked on you with the greatest favour! These persons have been very distressed and said it a great pity that you have wasted all this." The letter ends with the reproach that Dr. Michels used his house, of which Professor Fisher was the acting landlord, so badly that the house had still not been sold!

The reproduction of these statements is not intended to put the writer of the letter in a personally poor light. On the contrary, I am, unfortunately, rather certain that—except for the last sentence which is irrelevant to this discussion, unless the landlord's " good conduct certificate " was to be taken into account in the habilitation proceeding—the content of this letter would be regarded in most academic circles as quite in order. It is characteristic of our public life in general and of the situation in our universities in particular. I cannot honestly hide the fact that it is my " personal " conviction that the existence and the influence of such views, because indeed of their very sincerity, are no honour for Germany and its culture, and that furthermore as long as such views prevail it will be impossible—as far as I am concerned—to act as if we possess an "academic freedom " which someone could infringe.

I am convinced too—once again according to my own personal conviction—that religious communities, which knowingly and openly allow their sacraments to be used, in the same way as university fraternities and reserve officers' commissions are used—to make a career—richly deserve that contempt about which they frequently complain. I believe that Professor Amira, with his demonstrated sense of independence, would take the same view. In any case, it should be required in the interest of good taste and truthfulness that henceforward we ought not to speak of the existence of " the freedom of science and teaching " in Germany, as has always been done. The fact is that the alleged academic freedom is obviously bound up with the espousal of certain views which are politically acceptable in court circles and in salons, and furthermore with the manifestation of a certain minimum of conformity with ecclesiastical opinion or, at least, a facsimile thereof. *The " freedom of science " exists in Germany within the limits of political and ecclesiastical acceptability.* Outside these limits, there is none. Perhaps this is inseparably bound up with the dynastic character of our system of government. If it is, it should be honourably admitted, but we should not delude ourselves that we in Germany possess the same freedom of scientific and scholarly teaching which is taken for granted in countries like Italy.

V

THE ACADEMIC FREEDOM OF THE UNIVERSITIES [17]

THE discussions at the second conference of German teachers in institutions of higher education in Jena about academic freedom were unable really to clarify this difficult but nonetheless fundamental problem. Like much which has been said about this subject in recent years, the assembled university teachers at the conference were far too exclusively concerned with the " professional interests " of those persons who have already become university teachers. This is the only explanation for the assumption, made in all seriousness, that it is possible to separate the question as to whether a university teacher's expression of a particular belief, *e.g.*, a politically or religiously " radical " belief, should prevent his retention of a professorial chair—to which the answer was naturally negative—from the other question as to whether the same sort of belief should stand in the way of appointment to a professorial chair.

There is another equally widely shared view which asserts that the university teacher must, on the one side, " bear in mind " that he is an " official " when he acts publicly—as a citizen in elections, in statements in the press, etc.—but that, on the other side, he is entitled to claim the right that his statements in university classes are communicated no further. (Professor Schmoller has, as is known, successfully brought a legal action against a student who repeated outside things which had been said in one of his lectures.) If one links this latter viewpoint with the proposition that there is a significant difference between not permitting a professor to retain his chair and not allowing a person to be appointed to a chair when the disqualifying views are identical, one arrives at the following rather unusual conception of " academic freedom ": (1) when an appointment is at issue, not only the scientific or scholarly qualifications of the candidate for an academic post may and should be examined, but also his submissiveness to the prevailing political authorities and ecclesiastical usages; (2) a public protest against the prevailing political system may justify the removal of the incumbent of a professorial chair from his post; and (3) in the lecture hall, where neither publicity nor criticism are allowed, the persons who have been

[17] "Die Lehrfreiheit der Universitäten ", *Hochschul-Nachrichten*, XIX, 4 (January 1909), pp. 89–91. Max Weber wrote the above article on the invitation of the editor of *Hochschul-Nachrichten* after he had printed " Sozialdemokraten im akademischen Lehramte " (XIX, 1, October 1907, pp. 1–2) by Professor Conrad Bornhak of Berlin. Bornhak had taken an extremely hostile attitude towards the demand for academic freedom; he argued that the task of the universities was to train young persons for the service of state and church, and that socialists could not be entrusted with this task because they were enemies of the German social and political order and were determined to undermine it. Concerning *Hochschul-Nachrichten*, see *infra*, p. 33, fn. 27. [Editor.]

appointed as university teachers may express themselves as they wish "independently of all authority".

One sees that this conception of academic freedom would be ideal for one "whose wants are satiated" or for the "happy possessor of manifold goods" (*beati possidentes*), to whom neither the freedom of science and scholarship as such, nor the civil rights and duties of the university teacher have any significance; it is the ideal of those who wish to be at ease in the cultivation of the "station in life" in which they find themselves. And this "freedom" can naturally serve as a "fig-leaf" to cover up, to the greatest extent possible, the imparting of a certain political tone to university teaching in all those fields in which it is feasible. It is necessary to do no more here than indicate how much this view endangers the character of the aspirant to habilitation.

To this, we need only say: Society as a whole has no interest in guaranteeing the permanent tenure of a professorial corps which has been carefully screened to determine that its political views are unexceptionable and that, at least externally, its ecclesiastical views are no less unexceptionable.

"The freedom of science, scholarship and teaching" in a university certainly does not exist where appointment to a teaching post is made dependent on the possession—or simulation—of a point of view which is "acceptable in the highest circles" of church and state. In order to speak seriously of such "freedom", the first condition which must obviously be met is that both appointment to and continued tenure in a chair must be decided by the same criteria. Activities which according to the existing laws can constitute grounds for the removal, by judicial action or by a disciplinary committee, from his post of anyone who is a university teacher can of course also constitute grounds for refusing him the right to habilitate. If, however, that criterion does not apply in the former case, then it surely should not apply in the latter either. One might certainly put forth the argument that a punishable action—*e.g.*, an action of a political character—which provides grounds for disqualifying a professor from holding the "official" post of a professorship does not preclude admission to the status of a *Privatdozent*, since that is not an "official" appointment. But the entirely opposite proposition—which was repeatedly asserted in Jena [18]—namely, that no one can be disqualified from holding his official appointment as a professor, on account of an action which would disqualify a person from admission to the status of a *Privatdozent*, is a simple monstrosity. Only when this perfectly obvious point has been acknowledged can one begin to discuss the question as to which kinds of actions—public or private—may be regarded as incompatible with the role of a university teacher. I have a few observations to make on this point, with regard to a view which contends that the formal, legal character of the university as a state institution implies a criterion for academic appointment. In foreign universities, there are full professors who are, for example, socialists and, what is more, socialists of the most radical sort; some of them are among the most distinguished scientists and scholars of which the countries in question can boast. In Germany, the person who—according to the shifting currents of power and

[18] At the conference of university teachers. [Editor.]

opinion in the prevailing political " cartels ", " blocs " or " coalitions "—is regarded as an " enemy of the empire " has everything against him, while the person who is regarded by the political police as " dangerous to the state " is prevented from being appointed to a professorial chair by virtue of the legal right of control which officials can exercise—by requiring either a testimonial regarding political soundness before admission, or confirmation of admission by political officials following habilitation. But in addition to this, quite voluntarily, faculties usually function as deputies on behalf of the political police. All this happens just because the universities are supported financially and accorded privileges by the state—and despite the fact that the state regulates the examination of aspirants to positions in it as it pleases, and even though university training is only one training among many for appointment to the civil service and is not at all a claim to such an appointment. However, let us leave this formal mode of argument to one side and take up the " question " as it should be treated, namely, as an intellectual or cultural problem.

The fact that, in Germany, education in general, including higher education, is the concern of the state, results from a quite definite cultural development which is, on the one side, a consequence primarily of the secularisation of ecclesiastical lands, and on the other, of the deep, century-long poverty of the country. This prevented the growth of private foundations, which formed the basis of so many of the distinguished universities which have been built in the English-speaking countries. Today we must accept this as a fact to be taken into account in all our calculations and to the credit of which—we need not go further into this here—are many valuable features, since under the conditions which existed, the scale of the material resources made available to the universities could not have been provided except by the state. Naturally, this says nothing about the problem of how this development of the material foundations of our university system is ultimately to be assessed in the light of the totality of its accomplishments and effects.

If the " state ", *i.e.*, the seat of political power which dominates the national society, takes the view expressed in : " I sing the tune of him whose bread I eat ", if, in other words, the state conceives of the influence which it enjoys—in consequence of the economic situation of the universities—as a means of attaining a certain political obedience among university students, instead of looking upon it as an assumption of a cultural responsibility, then the interests of science and scholarship in such a " state " are no better and indeed, in many respects, are worse served than they were in the earlier condition of dependence on the church. The result of such a castration of the freedom and disinterestedness of university education, which prevents the development of persons of genuine character, cannot be compensated by the finest institutes, the largest lecture halls, or by ever so many dissertations, prize-winning works and examination successes. The favourite argument that the state—which means, it should be noted, the political group dominant at the moment—" cannot agree to allow " the universities to propagate " doctrines which are inimical to the state ", contains a fundamental error which, it cannot be denied, is also made in academic circles about the meaning and nature of university teaching in general. I shall now say a few words about this.

Universities do not have it as their task to teach any outlook or standpoint which is either " hostile to the state " or " friendly to the state ". They are not institutions for the inculcation of absolute or ultimate moral values. They analyse facts, their conditions, laws and interrelations; they analyse concepts, their logical presuppositions and content. They do not and they cannot teach what should happen—since this is a matter of ultimate personal values and beliefs, of a fundamental outlook, which cannot be " demonstrated " like a scientific proposition. Certainly the universities can teach their students about these fundamental outlooks, they can study their psychological origins, they can analyse their intellectual content and their most ultimate general postulates; they can analyse not what is demonstrable in them but what is believed—but they would be going beyond the boundaries of science and scholarship if they were to provide not only knowledge and understanding but also beliefs and " ideals ". What ideals the individual should serve—" what gods he must bow before "—these they require him to deal with on his own responsibility, and ultimately in accordance with his own conscience. The universities can sharpen the student's capacity to understand the actual conditions of his own exertions; they can teach the capacity to think clearly and " to know what one wants ". They are however in no way superior to a Jesuit academy, but rather are inferior to it, when they attempt to serve up, as science or scholarship, the personal beliefs and convictions of their teachers, or their political ideals—regardless of whether they are " radical ", either of the left or the right, or " moderate ". They are under the obligation to exercise self-restraint. The one element of any " genuine " ultimate outlook which they can legitimately offer their students to aid them in their path through life is the habit of accepting the obligation of intellectual integrity; this entails a relentless clarity about themselves. Everything else—the entire substance of his aspirations and goals—the individual must achieve for himself in confronting the tasks and problems of life.

It would be just as presumptuous for a university teacher to undertake, for example, to " demonstrate " the " justification " of certain social demands, as it would be for him to claim to " show ", by means of scientific or scholarly research, their " lack of justification ". Both of these are simply impossible with the means made available by science or scholarship. What science has to offer here is simply the analysis of the substance of those demands and the ultimate—neither demonstrable nor refutable—convictions and value-judgments on which they rest. It can discuss their historical origin and, further than that, the practical preconditions of their realisation and their predictable factual repercussions. Finally, it can offer some empirical understanding of whether present-day trends are moving in their direction or not, and why. These are all questions which are appropriate to " science and scholarship ". The individual's duty is to decide whether these ultimate beliefs should be accepted or rejected, whether he will be willing to take into the bargain those preconditions and repercussions of its realisation, or whether he will regard the costs as too great in relation to the chances of success. No university teacher can relieve him of this decision, nor should he do so, because these are not problems which can be settled scientifically.

Of course, it is unfortunately true that there are not a few university teachers—by no means predominantly "radical" politically but rather persons who are ostensibly "statesmanlike" conciliators—who fail to respect those obligations of self-restraint but assign to themselves the privilege, indeed the task, of educating their students into certain political beliefs and ultimate outlooks. By means of such arrogance, the universities will cut their own throats—for this conception of the tasks of education cannot deny the demand that the person who is in most circumstances most closely concerned, namely, the father who sends his son to university at his own expense, should be assured that his own ultimate outlook should be the one proposed. Religious, economic, social and political parties would then all possess the right to have separate universities or professorships provided for them, in which instruction in accordance with their own ideals would be given. Then, if one is to be consistent, it is necessary to accept the principle —more consistently carried out—of the Netherlands university reform scheme associated with the name of Kuyper, in accordance with which everyone has the right to establish a chair with all the privileges of the full professorship and, at the same time, an administrative office with the power of appointment. Then the Central Association of German Industrialists, the Monists' League, the Kepler League and the trade union confederation, as well as all the churches and political parties, could exercise this right, to the extent that they could supply the necessary funds. The Catholic and other churches in the Netherlands are already beginning to do this. This would be "academic freedom" in the field of "instruction in ultimate beliefs and values". If a person rejects such a conclusion, he must also honourably reject instruction in "ultimate values and beliefs" as a task for the university; he must also reject the consideration of the "ultimate values and beliefs" of a candidate as a criterion of academic appointment. He must look upon the establishment of professorial chairs—*e.g.*, in philosophy and history—which are intended quite explicitly to represent an ecclesiastical viewpoint, as a despicable violation of "the freedom of science"; but he must take the same attitude towards the rejection of a scientifically qualified candidate because he adheres to the "centre" or because he is a "socialist".

Cultural consensus in the field of education can be justified basically only on the condition of severe self-restraint in the observance of the canons of science and scholarship. If one desires this consensus, one must put aside the idea of any sort of instruction in ultimate values and beliefs; similarly the university teacher, especially in the confidentiality of his lecture hall— nowadays the object of such solicitude—is under the sternest obligation to avoid proposing his own position in the struggle of ideals. He must make his chair into a forum where the understanding of ultimate standpoints— alien to and diverging from his own—is fostered, rather than into an arena where he propagates his own ideals.

Only the theological faculties represent a purely historically conditioned

and apparent obstacle to the realisation of these demands. But this obstacle
does not rest on a question of principle. It is perfectly clear, if the university
is to maintain the character just delineated, which modes of discussion and
treatment of the phenomena of religious life belong in a university, and
which do not. The fact that these latter types of disciplines and the related
apologetic and practical specialties which can only be taught with dogmatic
commitment are now taught by state-appointed university teachers whose
academic freedom is thereby limited, instead of being taught by institutions
established by free religious communities, does not flow from any necessity
of the religious life, but rather solely from the desires of governmental bodies
concerned with the regulation of cultural and religious affairs. Awareness
that the strong religious communities, particularly the Roman Catholic
church, are already able to render wholly illusory the aim of this regulation
will, in association with the other motive forces of cultural development,
bring about the unavoidable separation. This will be in the interest of
religious life as well, and I hope that it will not be too late.

VI

AMERICAN AND GERMAN UNIVERSITIES [19]

THE main feature which strikes us when we confront the American
university system is its great qualitative and quantitative differentiation.
There are universities which are embryos at the beginning of their
development and there are others which are so differentiated and broad
in their provision of teaching that even large German universities cannot
compete with them. But universities in the United States are differentiated
in their qualitative characteristics and one may assert that this differentiation
is brought about essentially through a gradual and slow " Europeanisation "
of American university conditions. This Europeanisation will never lead
to identity with the European universities; it is nonetheless approximating
the German university, just as one may speak in many respects of an
" Americanisation " of Germany as far as academic matters are concerned.

The classic older type of American university grew out of the college.
Colleges were located not in large cities but wherever possible in the
countryside, in any case in small towns. Furthermore, the older colleges
were predominately established by religious sects. Traces of this can
be seen everywhere. Nowadays, however, American universities are
becoming to a certain extent metropolitan and, furthermore, there is no
doubt that at least in some of them the old collegiate system, with required
residence in college and strict control over the mode of life of the students,
is partly in process of being discarded and partly has already been discarded. At the same time, I have been assured in American business
circles that these latter conditions were responsible for maintaining the
college and the particular kind of college education, which does not aim

[19] Untitled address by Max Weber in *Verhandlungen des IV. Deutschen Hochschullehrer-tages zu Dresden am 12. und 13. October 1911* Bericht erstattet vom geschäftsfuhrenden Ausschuss (Leipzig: Verlag des Literarischen Zentralblattes für Deutschland (Eduard Avenarius], 1912), pp. 66–77.

primarily at training for science and scholarship, but rather at the
formation of character through the experience of holding one's own in
the society of similarly situated students, at the formation of adult citizens,
and at the development of an outlook which serves as the foundation of
the American governmental and social systems. All the while we find that
schools of economics [20] are being founded in Germany. To express ourselves in vivid form we may say that a driving force propelling these
schools of economics is the commercial employee's wish to attain the status
in which he may accept a challenge to a duel and thereby be made capable
of becoming a reserve officer: a pair of sabre scars on his face, a bit of
student life, a short rest from the habit of work—all things about which
I ask myself: will we be able to compete with the great productive
powers of the world, particularly the Americans, if the new generation of
our business class is educated into such an ethos?

The distinction between the American university and the German rests
to a considerable extent on the fact that the American universities are not
officially required to train young persons for examinations which will
qualify them for the governmental bureaucracy, for teaching in schools
and for I know not what else. In this respect, the American universities
are in an enviable position. I am however convinced that, with the
progress of administrative reform, sooner or later the time will come in
the United States when a somewhat similar situation will confront the
universities. I hope that they will be in a better position to protect their
independence and that they will be better placed to protect their most
sacred values than the German universities, through no fault of their
own, have been in the face of the great power of the state.

Let me touch briefly on the methods of teaching; Lamprecht says, with
a certain justification, that it would be hard for us to adopt these or to
learn from them. In themselves, these methods are very instructive. Here
we have to make a distinction between optional and required lectures. The
former are not distinguishable in any way from lectures in Germany
except for a much richer use of visual material. Those which I have heard
are no different from ours: matter of fact, precise, sober and without the
use of techniques which might stir crowds. The traditional and specifically
American type of required lectures for beginners differ markedly from
ours. The student is assigned the task of learning a given number of
sections of a textbook by a certain date; then he is questioned about the
content of these. This naturally can amount to an extremely lifeless type
of teaching. But I have also seen this method of instruction used at
Columbia University and elsewhere in a way which, in contrast with our
system of lectures and seminars, is a straightforward method of broad
instruction. Integral to this method of teaching is compulsory attendance
which is common in America.

Student life in America in general is very tangibly different from ours;
although European and particularly German influences are growing, it is
questionable whether these are of the best kind. When I was with American

[20] These institutions were primarily schools of business administration but they taught
the full range of economics, as it was then understood in Germany. They did not confer
degrees. [Editor.]

students nothing in the world interested them as much as learning about a German student duel. At Columbia University, I was invited to a proper German drinking bout, with sabres and all that goes with them, in the large auditorium in the university; it was staged by the German department of the university as part of an introduction to German culture.

The American student like the German student has his societies. These however are different from the German ones. The German societies are more like " insurance institutions " for providing useful connections and advancement in careers. One cannot assert that this element is entirely lacking in American student societies. One need only look into the publications of the boat clubs and the lists of old members to see that in such and such a year Mr. Roosevelt was elected president. Nonetheless the whole pattern of activity within the societies is very different from ours nowadays with their house-owner qualities, their bureaucratic tone, and their drill on which so much depends. Common to both is their educational character which consists in the fact that the individual must hold his own in a circle of very sharply and relentlessly critical coevals. The American students' ideal of manliness differs widely from that of the German students and it is difficult to measure one by the other.

With this I come to the constitution of the American university. You must permit me a few suggestions, particularly with reference to the German situation.

The constitution of American universities and much else about them is affected by the fact that the American universities, to an even greater degree than the German, are institutions which compete with each other. The fact that in the city of Chicago there are two universities and, in the state of Illinois, a third, namely the state university, shows how things stand; what is more this competition is in principle completely free. The American universities compete in a quite relentless way against their sister institutions. They bear the characteristics of competitive institutions. Like the modern industrial enterprise they pursue a policy of relentless selection with regard to proficiency, at least among their younger teachers. It is infinitely more thoroughgoing than can be found in any German university.

The decisive question which we should consider is a comparison of American and German universities with respect to their relations to the bureaucracy. This is something which is very close to our hearts in Germany. The German universities have been for a long time—sometimes latently, sometimes overtly—involved in the conflict between the traditional university authorities and the state bureaucracy which stands above them. This governmental bureaucracy in Germany is formally not unitary. University power rests in the hands of the individual states and it differs qualitatively in its entire character from one state which administers universities to every other one. The two university bureaucracies of Saxony and Baden are ahead of all others in their benevolence and in their understanding regard for the desires of the universities, even when they appear to them at first glance to be irrational and foolish, and even when they are perhaps actually foolish. For many years these two administrations have been, as I know from my own experience, quite different from the

administration in Prussia. They also seem to differ from the university administration in Bavaria—at least so it is said.

I confess quite openly that when I left the dominion of the Prussian educational administration for Baden I had the feeling of going into fresh air. German educational administrations have formed something like a cartel which has to a considerable degree annulled this competitive relationship. The cartel is obviously very much like the German railway association which is being formed, in the sense that the other educational administrations are becoming vassals of the Prussian university administration. Whose brain-child this cartel is became plain when I was called from Prussia to Baden. The entire correspondence which the Ministry of Baden had conducted with the Prussian Ministry was presented to me by the head of the university department of the Prussian Ministry, who questioned whether I would be inclined to accept an invitation from a " bloke "—I soften the term somewhat—who wrote such letters about me. The opposite of this would be unimaginable.

It is impossible to speak about these matters without touching on the personality who created the present-day system of Prussian and thereby of German educational administration. I refer to the late ministerial director Althoff.[21] It is very difficult to speak about this man. He was not

---

[21] Friedrich Althoff was born in 1839. After a short period of service in the imperial administration of the recently conquered territory of Alsace-Lorraine, in 1872 he became associate professor of law at the newly opened University of Strassburg. In 1880 he became full professor. In 1882 he accepted the post of rapporteur for academic personnel in the Prussian Ministry of Education. In 1897 he became ministerial-director of the Ministry with responsibility for all other sections of higher education as well as for universities. He continued in that office until his retirement in 1907. He died in 1908.

The Prussian universities flourished quantitatively under his administration. When he entered the Ministry in 1881–82, the appropriation for the Prussian universities for recurrent expenses was Mk. 7,573,775; when he became ministerial-director (1897–98), the appropriation rose to Mk. 11,662,343; in the year of his retirement (1907–08) it came to Mk. 16,647,269. Other categories of expenditure for the universities rose on approximately the same scale. A special fund for the "attraction and retention of distinguished teachers" rose from Mk. 98,864 at the beginning to Mk. 225,000 at the end of his period of service.

Rudolf Lehmann who admired Althoff wrote of him: "He who contributed so much to the universities also demanded a corresponding measure of influence. In part he was impelled by his driving personal will to power, his feeling of power, which came to life in dominating and influencing others. In larger part, however, it was his sense of being a representative of the state, who did not want to see any diminution of the power and privileges of the ruler who entrusted him with his powers, but who rather wished to extend those powers and privileges. He had the sense of superiority of the person who governs, who sees his territory in a large perspective and who guards against special interests on behalf of the whole. He did not wish to break the autonomy of the universities for the benefit of the sovereign authority, but he wanted to see the officials share in the making of decisions in all the more important matters in the administration of universities. As a result, and above all, what was most held against him was the procedure he adopted in the making of academic appointments. He did not go so far as to aspire to reduce the system of autonomous appointment by the faculties to a mere form and to replace it by appointments made by the state. . . . As a matter of fact, he not only adhered to the proper forms in dealing with the faculties but he also took their votes into very careful consideration; where they diverged from his own desires, he attempted to exercise influence by negotiations which he carried on officially with the faculty as a whole or with individual members in personal conversations. In these negotiations he used various means of pressure, some more stringent, some a bit milder." Lehmann, Rudolf: "*Der Unterricht bis zum Weltkrieg, 1892–1914*". Supplement to Paulsen, Friedrich, *Geschichte des gelehrten Unterrichts auf den deutschen Schulen und Universitäten vom Ausgang des Mittelalters bis zur Gegenwart*, third enlarged edition edited with a supplement by Rudolf Lehmann (Berlin

only a good human being in the specific sense of the word but he was also a man of very large perspectives. He could indeed say of himself: I see things more broadly than the gentlemen at the individual universities. On whether the present-day Prussian Minister of Culture could seriously say this of himself, I will remain silent. Furthermore, the German universities owe things to Althoff which are in a certain sense of permanent value. He was inspired by a degree of departmental patriotism of a sort which is hard to imagine in a more thoroughgoing form. He once said to me: " When I go to Minister Miquel, I will in future always carry a pistol with me, otherwise I won't be able to get any money from him to meet the needs of the universities." He raised the Prussian universities to an extraordinarily high level in technical respects, and in everything involving administrative resources and institutes. And in matters of personnel, it cannot be said too emphatically that here too his " departmental patriotism ", his devotion to the ends he sought, was overriding. There was no room for nepotism where he was, certainly not in the sense in which it is ordinarily understood. He could of course make mistakes and he did in fact do so. But his choices were often much more brilliant choices than those of the German universities. One reservation must be stated: in dealing with questions of personnel, he assumed that everyone he dealt with was a scoundrel or at least an ordinary place-hunter.

Put yourselves in the situation of an impecunious young teacher who has recently been married or engaged and who for the first time has come into the domain of this very superior intellect, and you will agree with me that there would be a danger that the young man in question, if he were subjected for some time to this power, would be forced into the direction, even if only partially, of becoming what Althoff presumably wanted him to become. The powers which were available to the Prussian Ministry of Education were the most thorough imaginable, and the system through which these powers were exercised carried with it the danger of producing a new academic generation which no longer adhered to the old traditions of the German university. It was rather an approximation to an American type—not to the type of an American academic, but rather to the type of American who is active in the stock exchange. Althoff's system had a directly corrupting influence. You may well ask for examples. Very well, I shall provide some.

I personally am exceptionally grateful to Privy Counsellor Althoff for the way in which he helped me materially and psychologically beyond what my merits justified.[22] But my pleasure was diminished by the observation that

and Leipzig: Vereinigung wissenschaftlicher Verleger, Walter de Gruyter, 1921), Vol. II, p. 705. [Editor.]

[22] Marianne Weber, Max Weber's widow, in her biography of her husband, gave a more precise account of Weber's experience with Althoff on this occasion:

" Althoff took a genuine interest in the talented teacher and wished to retain him in Prussia, where he thought he would be the right successor to Goldschmidt. He did not however know whether the Berlin faculty would be willing to approve such a young scholar as the successor to an old one of such scholarly eminence. So counting on human weaknesses, he tried a variety of artifices and sought to keep Weber in Prussia by making all sorts of promises to him. He told the head of the university affairs department of Baden that Weber expected to make a great career in Prussia as a legal scholar and that he would use the post in Freiburg only as a ' stepping stone '. Weber assured him that this remarkable sponsorship was connected with the fact that my father was a National-Liberal member of the Reichstag. The head of the Ministry of Education occasionally referred to this personal connection in a tactless and unsubtle way, which caused my father to resign his membership in the budget committee. This was revealed—and I was not the only one who was pleased—when he was able to gain recognition for his achievements from a source other than the Prussian state.

You will acknowledge that procedures like these were bound to have a corrupting influence in parliament, and not only in parliament, because such influences were exercised by that office in many directions. You will recall a case—into which I shall not enter further but which I shall only touch on here—which raised so much dust in the University of Berlin last year. We who stood unanimously behind our dishonestly treated Berlin colleague, all regretted that a demand was made on this colleague to provide an " assurance " on behalf of another colleague who was a protégé of the Ministry. This is contrary to academic convention. But the system of " assurances " comes from the Prussian Ministry. I will say only a little more about this.

When under Althoff's administration university teachers were called to Prussia from other universities, this never occurred without part of the payment being made in " promissory notes ", with an assurance of advancement in some other university but above all in the University of Berlin. Had our Berlin colleagues arrived at the day when all these " promissory notes " had to be realised in public, all the assurances which had been made to them on the contingency of the deaths of colleagues would be thrown into their faces with the question: " Do you intend to live forever?" and they would have been ashamed to go on living. These were assurances which the Ministry had forced on them. I myself arrived at the astonishing situation in which I was to become an associate professor and had long been in contact with the faculty, when, at the end of a meeting with him, the department head in the Ministry went to great pains to thrust an assurance

he would never allow himself to be imposed on the faculty at the University of Berlin or at any other university; Althoff's reaction was ' This man Weber shows an excessive delicacy in personal matters '. When one day Althoff saw Weber's father in his capacity as a rapporteur of the budget committee, he raised the question with him; both father and son were deeply angered, obviously because they saw it as an attempt to strike a ' bargain '. When the Minister of Education of Baden sought information about Weber from Althoff and told him at the same time that ' the unusual proposal of the faculty had raised certain questions ', Althoff showed the confidential correspondence to the young man with the remark ' I would not go to a state in which the Minister of Education so clearly showed his *animus non possidendi* '. Weber wished to reserve his right to decide freely in the event that Althoff did not explicitly request him to remain. The latter then presented him with a promise *in writing* to propose him to the Berlin faculty without any obligation on Weber's part. Weber agreed. But when, on reaching home, he opened the envelope and saw an added paragraph which placed him under the obligation of refusing any subsequent invitations to professorships at other universities, Weber rejected it at once. By return of post he received a letter which withdrew the paragraph, asserting that it had been an error. The letter bore an earlier date to give the impression that it had been written before Weber's objection. Weber was always persuaded of the contrary. This and other events strengthened his conviction that this outstanding man, like Bismarck, would use any means to attain his end, and that for this purpose he would exploit dependence and moral weakness, thus confirming his fundamental contempt for human beings. Such use of other human beings as pawns—even for very worthwhile ends—was abhorrent to Weber and he could not condone it." Weber, Marianne, *Max Weber: Ein Lebensbild* (Tübingen: J. C. B. Mohr [Paul Siebeck], 1926), pp. 211–212. [Editor.]

into my hand. I did not know why, until on the way home, I noticed that in the assurance there was a supplementary obligation which I had not accepted and which had not been in it when I read it. That is by the way. The main point is that when he forced this " promissory note " into my hand, he was taking it for granted that I would be a man who would be dependent on him. Assurances by the Ministry from the one side, assurances by the teachers from the other!

Gentlemen, I have personal experience of this too. Exactly the same thing was being suggested to me as was suggested to the colleague whose name aroused so much attention last year, and whose acceptance of it led him on the downward path of weakness and irresoluteness. When I was to become an associate professor, a secret teaching programme was suggested to me and I asked the reason for it. I was told that it was because the two full professors involved would have voted against my appointment as an associate professor. An impropriety was being proposed to me. I said that the two gentlemen in question had known about me for a long time. In a situation in which a high ranking official of a Prussian ministry tries to get young men to do something of that kind, I will not cast a stone at one who is entrapped and then commits actions which, seen objectively and in the light of the ethical standards of the academic profession, are utterly reprehensible.

I will now bring these remarks to a close with the question: how do things stand in the United States in these matters? The United States have an Althoff at every university. The American university president is such a man. He administers the university, and everything which in Germany rarely happens without wire-pulling on the part of the Ministry of Education is a result of his efforts. His real power is very much greater than his official power. He is in a position to checkmate what we call the faculty by drawing upon the support, through the democratic constitution of the university, of the younger members of the teaching staff. I am told that this is especially true of the modern large universities. The difference, for the time being, is that countless Althoffs exist alongside each other, and the president of one university looks different to the president of others. It is certainly to be deplored that appointments by one university of young teachers at another university are not very frequent and are declining in frequency. The aim of the university presidents is rather to draw on their own younger generation when it comes to appointments at higher levels.

Now a few words about this younger generation. The bureaucratic nature of university administration has increased greatly in the United States, and this is accompanied by an ideal which I regret, but which is quite understandably affirmed by the majority of our own younger generation, namely, the guaranteed material security of the younger generation of teachers. American universities have to compete with one another. The reverse side of the bureaucratisation of the younger generation and of the circumstance that every young teacher in the United States receives a salary—indeed one which according to German standards is rather high for a teacher at the beginning of his career—is the fact that every young teacher is subject to not being re-appointed. The decision not to renew or extend the appointment of a younger university teacher is not made as frequently as it could be made; nonetheless it is made very often. Furthermore, in return for their salaries, the younger generation of American university teachers are required to carry a teaching burden of a magnitude which is unknown in Germany.

I occasionally ask myself but always to no purpose: how can a young American assistant make progress in his research under conditions in which the full professor teaches three hours weekly while he himself teaches many times that? The situation is just the opposite of what it is in Germany. One may very seriously ask the question whether, if we consider the progress of science and scholarship, the American or the German system is to be preferred. I will not render a judgement on this subject today, particularly since my own experience has been confined to only a few universities. We are not here required to resolve the question as to whether in principle we should do things like the Americans in this or that respect. I have rather limited myself to drawing a few comparisons between the two countries.

A REPLY TO MAX WEBER [23]

Berlin, 23 October

THE *Norddeutsche Allgemeine Zeitung* writes semi-officially:

Dr. Max Weber, honorary professor of the University of Heidelberg has, according to newspaper reports which he has not denied, recently launched a furious assault on the memory of the deceased Ministerial-Director, His Excellency Althoff, before a public assembly of university teachers in Dresden. In support of these attacks, he referred to oral statements allegedly made by Althoff and particularly to Althoff's conduct when Professor Weber was invited from Berlin to Freiburg in 1894. Such attacks cannot diminish the great merit of Althoff's accomplishments on behalf of the Prussian universities and the honour in which he is held in very large circles even after his death; they rather redound to the discredit of the attacker. In reply, we will limit ourselves to the publication of a letter contained in the archives of the Ministry for Religion and Education of the Archduchy of Baden; this letter was written by Althoff about Professor Weber in reply to an inquiry about him by the then head of the university affairs department of the Archduchy of Baden.

Berlin, 19 February, 1894

Very esteemed colleague,—In reply to your inquiry of the 10th of this month, I respectfully reply that Professor Weber, in the event of an invitation to Freiburg, will be allowed to have complete freedom of choice; it is not at all in our mind to claim that the fact that he has only recently become an associate professor has placed him under obligation to reject the invitation. If he, in contrast to others, has scruples about coming to a decision without prior consultation with his official superiors, that is certainly to his honour. It would not, therefore, accord with our practice to place any obstacle whatsoever in the way of his free decision. Professor Weber is a person who is so outstanding in every respect that we wish him only the best, and we could

---

[23] Untitled news item, *Frankfurter Zeitung* (*Morgenblatt*), 24 October, 1911.

in any case not assume the responsibility of encroaching on his own view as to what is best for his own development.

With highest regard, I remain,

Yours most devotedly,

ALTHOFF.

VII

MAX WEBER ON THE " ALTHOFF SYSTEM "[24]

PROFESSOR Max Weber has, as is known, spoken about Althoff at the conference of teachers in higher education in Dresden along the same lines as those on which he had spoken previously. The *Norddeutsche Allgemeine Zeitung* has dealt censoriously with Professor Weber and we have reported this in our main edition of 24 October. Now Professor Weber writes to us:

Dear Editor,—The *Norddeutsche Allgemeine Zeitung* has attempted to turn my attack on the method of dealing with human beings which still prevails in the Prussian Ministry of Education, and which in my opinion has a corrupting effect, into a personal attack against the late Privy Counsellor Althoff. It has shifted the issue from the present to the past and from a discussion of facts into personalities. To this end it publishes a letter from the gentleman in question to the previous head of the department of university affairs in the state of Baden; I knew of the existence and of the intention of this letter but not of its particular content. Now that the letter has been published I wish to make the following remarks:

(1) The letter contains a passage: " It would not therefore accord with our practice (i.e. that prevailing in Berlin) to place any obstacle whatsoever in the way of his (i.e., my) free decision "—although the Berlin practice was and is to place newly appointed teachers under the obligation by an assurance that they will not accept any outside invitations, and even though not so very long ago Privy Counsellor Althoff expressly attempted to place me under such an obligation through exactly that sort of assurance. That this attempt was made must at least to some extent be officially recorded since the letter which withdrew that request bore an official notation. The handwritten copy, and my letter to which reference was made, might perhaps be lacking in the archives; so too might a complete note of the content of the discussion to which reference is made in the letter. The details of these transactions are not relevant here.

(2) The letter contains some flattering remarks about myself. I cannot go into an exposition of the antecedents and intentions of this letter and will only say, in this regard, that Privy Counsellor Althoff, as was frequently evident to me, obstinately refused to believe in my repeated and emphatic declaration that I had an invitation to Baden and did not wish to drive a " bargain " regarding an arrangement which, as I foresaw, he intended, since I would either remain *without conditions* or leave *without conditions*. (His letter in that particular state of affairs almost

---

²⁴ " Max Weber über das ' System Althoff ' ", *Frankfurter Zeitung*, 27 October, 1911.

necessarily forced me to accept the invitation from Baden; it might indeed have been intended to do so.)

I will further remark that I see nothing in the mode of official evaluation and treatment of a teacher which must or should place him under an obligation of gratitude, since appointments and promotions should be governed, not by considerations of personal friendship, but by serious and realistic scientific, scholarly and educational considerations. Likewise, Althoff's friendly attitude toward me personally could not possibly place me under obligation to pass favourable judgment on his system, any more than—as I said in detail in Dresden—the mode in which it was expressed and the motives by which it was partly impelled could wound me. My gratitude was limited to these two points as Althoff—and this I repeat—must have known precisely. The way in which Schmoller [25] and Wagner [26] were treated by the present lords of this ministry in the " Bernhard affair " shows that, at least in the conduct of the Prussian educational administration, " gratitude " certainly does not pay; Gustav Schmoller and Adolf Wagner did more for the glorification of the Prussian monarchy and Prussian administration than all the officials of the Ministry of Culture together, while Schmoller for many decades supported those officials in the most difficult aspects of their work in such a way that one could almost say that he relieved them of the most crucial parts of their burdens.

It is simply not true that I have damaged Althoff's memory by what I have actually—and not just allegedly—said; I have emphatically acknowledged his merits and his purely personal qualities as well, both in public and in private. But we should not discuss only the cases cited as illustrations but rather the system which he created and which is still in operation. The system worked through assurances: (1) assurances by the teachers regarding all possible and impossible things, and by no means

[25] Gustav von Schmoller was born in 1838 and died in 1917. He began his career as a civil servant and then became professor at the University of Halle in 1864, at the University of Strassburg in 1872, and finally at the University of Berlin in 1882 where he remained until 1913. Although not a Prussian by origin, he became an ardent advocate of Prussia, being appointed official historian of Brandenburg and Prussia in 1887, a member of the Prussian state council in 1884, and a representative of the University of Berlin in the upper house of the Prussian Diet in 1885. He was a co-founder of the Verein für Sozialpolitik, an important organisation of academic social scientists seeking to promote social reforms. He was also the editor of several important series of publications on social, administrative and economic history, and editor after 1881, of the then leading German social science periodical *Jahrbuch für Gesetzgebung, Verwaltung and Volkswirtschaft*—subsequently known as *Schmoller's Jahrbuch*. He dominated German academic social science for many years and exercised great influence over academic appointments in that field. He was a *Kathedersozialist*—a " professorial socialist "; this entailed the rejection of economic liberalism and the assignment of a central role to the state in the regulation, management and operation of the economy. It also entailed an extensive programme of welfare legislation for the benefit of the working classes. All this was intended to strengthen the German imperial regime, to prevent the deleterious social effects of unrestrained capitalism, and to curb class conflict. He was deeply devoted to the monarchy and the Prussian civil service but also no less deeply concerned with the improvement of the condition of the working classes. [Editor.]

[26] Adolf Wagner was born in 1835 and died in 1917. In 1870, after having taught in the Universities of Vienna, Dorpat and Freiburg, he became professor of economics at the University of Berlin where he remained for 46 years. He was one of the first of the *Kathedersozialisten*. With Gustav Schmoller he was a co-founder of the Verein für Sozialpolitik. For a time he was a member of the lower house of the Prussian Diet in the conservative interest. In his time, in Germany, he was thought to be a very important economist. [Editor].

only the non-acceptance of " invitations " from other universities; and (2) assurances by the educational administration regarding such matters as prospects in the event of the death of full professors at Berlin and elsewhere, obligations of silence, conflict-generating intervention into the relations of colleagues, the subvention [27] and withdrawal of announcements of lectures according to taste, the " leaking " of official documents for the purpose of press campaigns, and all the things of which I actually spoke.

The prevailing system is attempting to transform our new academic generation into academic " operators ", into persons who will fit into this machinery without any further thought, but it actually produces conflicts of conscience and leads them into taking false steps, the consequences of which they will have to bear throughout their academic lives. A sober educational administration, the officials of which can cope with the dangers of the great power which they possess, can and must refrain from using such means. This is quite apart from the fact that the use of methods which were repeatedly pardoned in the case of Althoff can for that very reason no longer be tolerated in the case of others.

I finally request permission to repeat here that there were erroneous reports and misunderstandings in a large part of the press which dealt with the substance of my exposition, and that as a result the Baden ministry and two leading Berlin scholars were subjected to absolutely baseless suspicions. Meanwhile I have stated this publicly elsewhere. Since it is absolutely impossible to know how widely these errors have been broadcast in the press, and equally impossible to send corrections to the entire German press, may I here request other German newspapers to take note of these remarks?

Finally, I use this opportunity to make perhaps one additional observation. Here and there in the press, reference has been made—with unpleasant side glances at my colleagues—to the particular " courage " which I have shown in the open discussion of such matters. This is very unjust. When my colleagues, especially those in Prussia, take part in public discussions of such widely-known facts, they place at risk not only their personal positions but also the professional interests of their institutes, since they depend for their resources on the goodwill of the Ministry of Education. This is not so in my case since my relationship with the University of Heidelberg which, recalling earlier years, is very precious to me and which I might involve in an extreme case, is unfortunately for the present and the foreseeable future only a formal one. I certainly do not take the comfortable position with regard to the matters in question here that " such discussions can serve no purpose and so they should be avoided ".

With all respect,
PROFESSOR MAX WEBER

[27] This presumably referred to the problematic periodical of *Hochschul-Nachrichten*, a privately owned journal conducted by one Salvisberg who supported the government against the universities whenever they were in conflict. The government, in return, required after 1893 that all courses of lectures be announced in Salvisberg's journal; for these announcements a substantial fee had to be paid by the universities to the journal, the continued survival of which depended on its income from these compulsory advertisements. See Brentano, Lujo, *op. cit.*, p. 286. [Editor.]

34 *Max Weber*

A SECOND REPLY TO MAX WEBER

Max Weber and the " Althoff System " [28]

Berlin, 28 October

THE *Norddeutsche Allgemeine Zeitung* makes the following observations regarding the statements by Professor Max Weber (27 October, 1911):

We have no desire to become involved in further discussions with Professor Weber. He is however utterly wrong when he contends that there exists in the Prussian Ministry of Education a system of assurances of the most diverse sort. Those who have accepted appointments in the Prussian universities will corroborate this—and there are indeed many such in recent years. No assurances are required of professors when they accept an appointment. What is however required is that the following declaration be signed:

Declaration

On the occasion of my appointment at . . . I accept the obligation:
(1) Not to enter into negotiations regarding an appointment to another university or any other appointment without previously informing the Minister of Culture.
(2) To meet the outstanding obligations of my present appointment up to 1 October, or 1 April, and only after giving a prior notification of three months.
(3) In the case of acceptance of an appointment to another university within the first three years from 1 . . . . . . , I will repay Mk . . . which are the removal costs which had been granted me to cover the cost of moving; I will do this before my departure from . . . The sum will be paid to the university treasurer's office in that place. . . . . . . 19 . . .

The third obligation is required in all the German states, except that in certain university administrations the period during which the liability to repayment is valid is not three years but five.

(Professor Weber will undoubtedly reply.)

VIII

MAX WEBER AND THE ALTHOFF SYSTEM [29]

PROFESSOR Max Weber of Heidelberg writes us:

Dear Editor,—I would be grateful if you would print the following remarks on the statements made in the *Norddeutsche Allgemeine Zeitung* of 28 October [1911]. The *Norddeutsche Allgemeine Zeitung* has once more shifted the subject of discussion. The " declaration " which it prints and which is to be signed by all professors is obviously not an " assurance " of the type which I was discussing. The obligation which is contained in article 3 of the declaration was even accepted by me as

28 " Max Weber und das ' System Althoff ' ", *Frankfurter Zeitung*, 31 October, 1911.
29 " Max Weber und das System Althoff ", *Frankfurter Zeitung*, 2 November, 1911.

self-evident and unquestionable when I was invited to Baden. Articles 1 and 2 are utterly harmless. In contrast, the assurance which was desired of me contained the acknowledgement that I accepted the obligation to reject an " invitation " which might be extended to me to take up a post at another university. Since there was no mention of such a thing in the oral negotiations, I refused in writing to submit to such an unreasonable demand. When, however, the *Norddeutsche Allgemeine Zeitung* wishes to insist that assurances of exactly this type are alien to the system of the late Ministerial Director Althoff, this contention will undoubtedly surprise those numerous colleagues from whom such assurances have been demanded—partly successfully and partly unsuccessfully. If the observation is only intended to suggest that " in recent years "—as the *Norddeutsche Allgemeine Zeitung* puts it—this practice is no longer used, then it should be pointed out that the recent establishment of the cartel-like arrangements of state university administrations have rendered these procedures, which are objectionable to non-Prussian university administrations, inappropriate means to the end which is sought. I must make clear that I have expressly spoken not only about assurances of the just-mentioned indirectly offensive type. I have also spoken of assurances of the acceptance of the obligation to deliver lectures not on the official lecture list—which was proposed to me. I have also spoken about assurance of acceptance of the obligation of silence (such as had been suggested to me and to others and also, what is more, quite recently) which is a clear infringement on the existing law of corporations. I have also spoken of assurances against appearances at public meetings— exactly this happened in a manner well known to me, although many years earlier. I have further discussed assurances given by the educational administration regarding opportunities for professorships which would become vacant as a result of death or retirement of certain full professors at the major universities. The Althoff administration was very liberal in paying with these " promissory notes " when it made appointments to Prussian universities; I am still waiting for the announcement that similar offers have not been made in recent years. These assurances were—in cases known to me—made in writing. Since the *Norddeutsche Allgemeine Zeitung* asserts that it has no occasion to engage in further discussion with me, I will simply observe that, from the very start, I have not felt any need to engage in such inevitably fruitless discussions with this newspaper. I only want to call attention once more to the fact that my observations were made in the first instance with reference to certain publicly-known events of very recent occurrence, and that the citation of a few examples which lie further back in the past was simply intended to illustrate the working of the system.

May I supplement my observations about the schools of economics which I corrected elsewhere in detail? Letters sent to me privately as well as letters from principals of schools of economics show that, in spite of that analysis, my statements are still regarded as " derogatory " of their activities. May I also say that I have the impression that at least in Cologne my apprehensions regarding the influence of the student societies, which in my view are wholly out of place in schools of

economics, have been seen as baseless. In view of this, I shall return to
these points in a letter which I am sending shortly to the directors of the
schools of economics in question. In this letter, I will state for whatever
use anyone wishes to make of them the facts on which I base my views;
these have come to me, orally and in writing, from circles about whose
detachment and information I cannot be in doubt.

With highest regard,
PROFESSOR MAX WEBER

IX

THE SCHOOLS OF ECONOMICS [30]

THE well known address by Professor Max Weber has been answered in
three contributed articles. Following the articles by two representatives of
the Berlin School of Economics—the rector, Professor Binz, and Professor
Paul Eltzbacher—and a representative of Leipzig University, Professor Ludwig
Beer, we are now publishing a statement which Professor Max Weber has
sent us.

A REPLY

Without inquiring of me whether a report which was widely published
in the press regarding a statement which I made about schools of economics was correctly and fully reproduced, two professors including,
regrettably, the rector of the Berlin School of Economics have attacked
me in the *Berliner Tageblatt*. They at least had the decency, shown by
few others, to send me their critical remarks. In view of the haste with
which these gentlemen so energetically took up the " defence " of the
schools of economics, I, as a result of being away from here and being
overburdened with unavoidable tasks, did not feel it necessary to rush
immediately to a public correction, especially since I had informed both
of my critics that the press account had given an incorrect impression of
my address. The errors arose from the fact that the reporters, obviously
because of lack of space, thought themselves compelled to amalgamate
not only several sentences, but sentences from two different talks into a
single sentence containing what they thought to be essential. At the end
of the proceedings, I took pains expressly and emphatically to make it
clear that I am extremely well aware of the excellent work by our—in
part—very outstanding colleagues at the schools of economics. I read
very carefully those reports which are available to me regarding the
schools of economics, especially the one in Cologne. Since moreover the
school of economics in Berlin is primarily the accomplishment of my
former Berlin colleague, I. Jastrow, while those in Cologne and Mannheim
owe their establishment to my present colleague, E. Gothein, and since
moreover, to mention no others, my friend and editorial colleague,
Werner Sombart, teaches in Berlin, even the most ill-informed rector

[30] " Die Handelshochschulen: Eine Entgegnung ", *Berliner Tageblatt und Handels-
Zeitung*, 27 October, 1911.

might have thought it proper to address me directly before making a public statement. Had he immediately sent me the issue of the *Berliner Tageblatt* of 14 October, he would have had my answer on his desk on the day he sent off his manuscript to the paper (16 October). I attach great importance to replying in this same newspaper.

In the course of a comparison in Dresden of American and German conditions I said—partly by implication and partly literally—referring to the point which is relevant here: In America, a dual tendency may be seen in the traditional " college " (which combines student residence with a " humanistic " course of study at the level of the *Prima* of our *Gymnasium* and the first semesters of work in our philosophical faculties). One of these tendencies is the development of specialised studies along European lines. This tends to reduce that institution to a lesser role as a constituent part of the traditional university—in Baltimore, for example, there is already a *Gymnasium* on the German pattern as an institution preparatory to the university. There is another quite opposite tendency found in American business circles—so I was repeatedly told, to my surprise—although I could not assess how widespread this tendency is or how enduring it will be. According to this view, the college, with its particular impact on the character—in the sense of the Anglo-Saxon ideal of the " gentleman "—and the particular type of general education which it offers, seems, according to the experience of these circles, a setting especially adapted for education towards independence—and, it should be added, for the healthy civil self-respect of the embryonic businessman, both as a human being and in his job; as such it is better than a specialised course of study. To be sure the growing appreciation of degrees by these circles is one of those phenomena of " Europeanisation " which is affecting all American life, not only academic life, and will go even further with the reform of the civil service.

I should add that the mode of attainment and the practical significance of academic degrees differ in important respects in the United States and Germany. In Germany, similar ends are sought through the establishment of schools of economics. The reason for the creation of separate institutions for this purpose is, on the one hand—a point which I emphasised—to be found in the pride of our traditional universities. " Think of the shudder of an average privy-counsellor-professor of law if he were expected to sit in the meeting of a faculty of law or political science with a person representing a subject of such low status as business administration or accounting." I should say here that I regard it as unfortunate that evidence of a fundamental study of these subjects is not required of candidates in economics in the universities.

Another major reason for the separate establishment of schools of economics is the undeniable existence—I did not say " universal " or even " preponderant "—among the new generation of businessmen both in commerce and industry, of a desire for that feudal type of prestige which is conferred by wearing the colours of a student society, sabre cuts, and above all by the qualification for giving " satisfaction " in a duel and hence for becoming a reserve officer, which is acquired through the traditional form of student life which is led at the cost of intensive study.

In the notes I made before my talk but which, perhaps in the excitement of speaking, I forgot, I also said that if these tendencies and the pressure for the creation of new types of official degrees and diplomas (which is expanding in all occupations on a Chinese scale) increase, it will not be a lasting advantage to us in our economic competition with the great industrial powers of the world. This is what I said. I made a comparison and described the conflicting tendencies as well as the weaknesses of the two countries, and I went into some detail in dealing with the American universities and colleges in other respects. I could not remain silent about these things, and I had to take it for granted that in the audience which I was addressing it was well enough known that I would not make a foolish remark to the effect that the students of the schools of economics were preponderantly—or even exclusively—persons with that feudal ambition; or that I would contend that there were only "colour-students" at the universities, although everyone knows these students are in a very influential minority.

Now for a brief tale: One day there appeared in the office of a firm making ready-made goods a travelling salesman of a firm supplying semi-finished products—a gentleman whose appearance was only equalled by the perfection of the content of his visiting card. The latter read: "X, Lieutenant of the Reserve", etc.; at the bottom left it said, "D and Co."; at the bottom right, it gave the address. The partner of the firm who was in the office expressed his regret that the visit had not been announced by telephone, as was customary for all the suppliers since it enabled them to deal more expeditiously with the business at hand. He could not ask his partner who had to deal with such decisions to leave the work he was doing at the moment which could not be put aside. He suggested that the salesman return at another hour. Moreover he felt it necessary to call the salesman's attention to two things: the first was that the most recently delivered goods had not been of a sufficiently high quality, and the other was that the prices asked were demonstrably bettered by competitors. The elegantly nasal reply was, almost literally: "I re-gret ve-ry much that you think that your partner who, as far as I know, has an officer's qualifications, does not regard it as necessary to greet a com-rade at once. Furthermore you should regard the fact that I am a reserve officer as sufficient evidence that I supply only high grade goods at the best prices. I re-gret it ve-ry much." Elegant and dignified withdrawal.

It certainly does not occur to me to blame schools of economics for this type of travelling salesman, about whom the dumbfounded manufacturer is still laughing and who could scarcely produce very brilliant results for his firm. I will however say that when I told this little story to a gentleman with quite other connections he said: "This is not by any means rare. Many suppliers seriously think that they will make a good impression through such salesmen and, sometimes, on the first occasion, they actually succeed in doing so because those who have to deal with this type of salesman are bewildered by the task of getting rid of such an unusual figure, and therefore place an order for a shipment of (unusable goods—but this never happens a second time."

I add that this anecdote illustrates, certainly in an uncomfortable way, the tendencies which would be nurtured or strengthened in the new generation of our businessmen in commerce and industry, if such persons, equipped with degrees and hence putting on airs of social superiority to their colleagues, begin to turn up frequently in our firms, and if the qualities which are fostered in student societies or the type of feudal pretensions which are all too easily encouraged by the symbols of military qualification become much more prominent. This is not the place to discuss in what sense the student societies—about which I did not speak as generally as has been asserted—and the military have an " educational " impact. But neither the possession of a coloured ribbon nor the possession of an officer's commission is as such proof that its possessors can do the hard and serious work without which the industrial and commercial bourgeoisie cannot maintain Germany's position in the world. Since I have been accused in one paper of taking a contemptuous view of " clerks ", let me say that my name comes from a Westphalian linen family and that I do not deny my pride in this bourgeois descent, unlike the groups of which I spoke, who do so only too readily.

Without touching on the other schools of economics, let me say without qualification that the well known prohibition of the ridiculous nonsense of the student societies at the Berlin School of Economics was a very wise action. The decision, which dealt with only one feature of this whole complex, is closely associated with the generally independent character which that institution has in many respects shown since its origin, and which has caused difficulties for the men who created it and for the school itself in its early years. Some of these difficulties came from certain circles in German industry which have an inclination towards the espousal of feudal ideals.

X

REMARKS SUPPLEMENTING THE TALK AT DRESDEN [31]

YESTERDAY, your report of 14 October on my talk before the Deutschen Hochschullehrertag reached me. The report contains a number of errors which in large measure are similar to those which I am told appeared in other newspapers. Their origin must be partly attributable to mishearing what I said and partly to inevitable compression leading to the omission of sentences such as probably appeared of minor interest to your reporters. I must however lay some stress on these missing sentences, since your account has put some particularly outstanding scholars of the University of Berlin in a light which I would not allow for a moment to remain uncontradicted.

(1) In your account, you attribute to me the statement " When I was invited from Prussia to Baden, there was laid before me in Baden, the entire correspondence which Prussia had conducted with the Ministry in Baden, and I read there what had been written about me in Prussia. The

---

[31] " Professor Max Weber über seine Rede auf dem Deutschen Hochschultagung zu Dresden ", *Tägliche Rundschau*, 22 October 1911.

head of the department in Baden asked me how I could have once accepted an " invitation from a bloke who wrote about me in this way '." This is a simple confusion, which is undoubtedly a result of a mistake in hearing. The actual facts were just the opposite. They were as follows. Before my invitation to Baden was settled, there was correspondence between the then head of the department in Baden and the then Prussian departmental head, Privy Counsellor Althoff. The Baden official inquired whether certain information which I had given to the faculty in Freiburg at their request was actually correct. Privy Counsellor Althoff let me know of this inquiry and then asked me whether I thought I could honourably accept an invitation from a " bloke " who doubted my statements. The Baden department head explained on another occasion that the government of his state was in a position where it had to decide between the Freiburg faculty, which was repeatedly pressing for my appointment, and such and such—purely practical—considerations which were against my appointment, particularly the question as to whether I would not do better to remain in Berlin. (It would serve no purpose here to go into these considerations.) Privy Counsellor Althoff in this connection asked whether I thought I could accept an invitation from a " creature " who showed an *animus non possidendi* towards me and who had corresponded with him in that way.

I told him in the first instance that I did not feel insulted by the request of a government department for official confirmation of information given to it by a private citizen; in the second case, I replied that the investigation in question—in so far as it was in agreement with statements which I had made to the Freiburg faculty when they declared their intention to propose me to the Ministry—was not insulting but that for me the confidence of the colleagues with whom I would have to work was my primary concern. The further details are irrelevant in clearing up this misunderstanding.

I did not mention these details, which I could amplify, at the university teachers' conference, but only the fact that the head of the Prussian university affairs department wanted me to look through the correspondence which his colleague from Baden had addressed to him about me and which had been disdainfully annotated. He also asked me what he should answer. I mentioned the experience in order to illustrate the manner in which the university administrators of the other German states —as your account reports—were treated by Prussia under the influence of the well known cartel-like arrangement.

In the last sentence of your report you assert that I gave " high and holy assurances " that I could support my statements by letters. That was a mistake in hearing. Those present, in so far as they were able to hear what I said, will confirm that I said we could speak of " documentary " proof of this purely personal conversation only in the sense that I could reproduce the content of these letters with a fairly high degree of accuracy. Whether these letters, handwritten on octavo size paper by *Oberregierungsrat* Arnsperger, can be found in the official files, or were treated by Privy Counsellor Althoff as private correspondence, I have no way of knowing. (To my great regret I have only now learned that the head of the Baden department, who later assumed another post, has died.)

(2) The second point concerns the following sentence in your report: "It went so far that as a result of the tactless and insolent manner in which the departmental head of the Ministry of Education took these personal relations—between myself and my father who was then a member of the Reichstag—into account, my father resigned his position on the parliamentary budget committee." I add for the sake of precision that my father was rapporteur for parts of the budget. At a parliamentary meeting, Privy Counsellor Althoff suggested that my father should consult me—I was at that time a *Privatdozent*—about whether it was worthwhile to authorise a certain newly proposed professorship of economics—which is of no interest here—before he agreed to its expected rejection by the National-Liberal faction. My father explained to me, after a long discussion and with my strong agreement, that he did not feel that he should serve as rapporteur any longer. Althoff's statement was so formulated that no direct step could be taken against him, but in substance his intention was perfectly clear. I have gone into considerable detail here in order to clear up all ambiguities.

(3) Your report mentions the following statement by me:

I too have been pressed to give an assurance, in accordance with which I would be assigned to teach without an official programme. When I asked the reason I was told that the teaching programme must remain secret because Professors Brunner and Gierke [32] would vote against my appointment. Thus a direct act of impropriety was proposed to me.

This is incomplete and not quite correct. I added to my Dresden talk an account of my refusal to sign an assurance that I would lecture on Germanic subjects as well as on those subjects stipulated in my terms of appointment. I also said that with regard to the secrecy of the proceedings and its reasons, Herr Althoff remarked that the two specialists on German law and institutions, Brunner and Gierke, had already voted for my nomination in the faculty, although they (and the dean) had been precisely informed by me that I intended to give those lectures. Privy Counsellor Althoff said "Then the matter is settled" and he made a few pencilled notes.

I have mentioned what happened in the negotiations in order to show how that contemptuous attitude towards even our most eminent scholars, and the fact that such suspicions were laid before one of our younger Berlin colleagues by the head of the personnel section, has had a corrupting influence on the new academic generation. I also had the intention of illuminating the conditions under which the so-called "Bernhard affair", for example, arose. Professor Bernhard's failure immediately to recognise what, from his colleague's standpoint, was the impropriety of accepting the obligation of silence in connection with a promise of government which infringed the law of the university, led him inescapably into a situation, which despite the brilliance of his external position, will certainly not be envied by any colleague.

[32] Heinrich Brunner and Otto von Gierke were the two leading historians of medieval German law and institutions. [Editor.]

Enough of this. Permit me to make two observations. It was obviously not fitting that I should speak continuously about myself in a public gathering. I have however been informed confidentially about innumerable similar experiences by others, which I cannot mention publicly or privately under any circumstances and despite the danger that persons who do not know me will not believe me. But there is nothing I can do to persuade them that I have the evidence.

It might be asked why did I not mention these things when Althoff was alive. To this I reply that when the famous dinner for Althoff was being arranged, I consulted several colleagues in order to bring these and similar matters into public view. We thought we should do this in order to defend the criticism which the late Professor Michaelis directed against the Althoff system—in our view it went astray on a few points but was right in others. This criticism has been described by Professor Schmoller as "shocking" and it was our desire to respond to this judgement. At that time Professor Michaelis was personally completely unknown to me. We concluded that, in spite of everything, Althoff was preferable to his prospective official successors and that such things should be left untouched. My decision to adduce the support of examples for the doubts which I had publicly expressed when the future Frankfurt university was surrendered to the Prussian bureaucracy—at that time it was said that my arguments had to be supported by examples—was arrived at largely because the Prussian Minister of Education, who had only taken office a little while before, thought he was justified in Breslau in publicly praising his bureaucracy and that, after what had happened in the preceding year, at the expense of the universities. Another important consideration in making my decision was the way in which the Prussian educational administration had proceeded in dealing with three eminent colleagues at the University of Berlin in connection with the Bernhard affair.

The officials of the Ministry of Education released to a section of the press information which they possessed only in an official capacity, in order to promote a press crusade of the most despicable sort against the three colleagues. No one in Berlin who is aware of these events doubts that it was the gentlemen of the Ministry of Education who incited or at least supported Professor Bernhard in undertaking actions which the court of arbitration characterised as perfidious; the bureaucrats had felt themselves called upon to play the judge in a dispute in which they were one of the parties.

It is also clear that the Prussian Ministry of Education used public funds to pay for announcing lectures which on the one side was super-fluous according to Vornflach,[33] and for withdrawing the same announcements on the other; for materially chastising four independent men who were not of the same opinion as they were; for subsidising toadies and informers who saw their task as besmirching professors who were uncongenial to their superiors. I have not wished to attack the Minister of Education and his officials personally nor to criticise their professional

---

[33] The identity of Vornflach is unknown to me. The announcement and cancellation of lectures appears to refer to the ministerial practice of requiring lecture courses to be advertised, for payment, in *Hochschul-Nachrichten*. [Editor.]

scrupulousness, but only to point out the continuation of a system which in their hands shows all the weaknesses and none of the strengths which, I have explicitly acknowledged, it exhibited when in the hands of its founding genius, Privy Counsellor Althoff. Your report acknowledges that I have done justice to Althoff's personal and professional merits.

Althoff knew my personal view of his system—I never sought him out of my own free will—through my direct comments at our first detailed discussion, as well as through the dean of the Berlin faculty of law, whom I asked to explain to him more clearly than I had done that certain of his remarks—about colleagues of my own generation—were absolutely intolerable. He also knew of my views through a third person who was close to him. I often entertained my friends by telling them of his grotesque answers. He never came into very close personal contact with me. One had to take him personally as he was, and when he retired I thanked him only in writing for his help, without finding his system any more forgivable; he himself knew I found it intolerable. His most decisive flaw was his open and unqualified contempt for other human beings. At Dresden, with the vigorous agreement of the audience, I emphasised that this was responsible for much that has occurred within the universities. But I also had to point out that as other better administered states show, university affairs are conducted as well without that deceitful cunning from which everyone who had to deal with him suffered. At Dresden I adduced an example of this which was not mentioned in your report. This underhand conduct could not really produce a wholesome effect on the new academic generation. In order to clarify a misunderstanding of our colleague Kaufmann, I must say that whenever I had to deal with the ministry in Baden I always felt that I was breathing "fresh air".

XI

THE "ALTHOFF SYSTEM" ONCE AGAIN [34]

PROFESSOR Max Weber in Heidelberg writes us:

Dear Editor—May I once more—I think, for the last time—request the hospitality of your pages?

I neither sought nor wished to provoke any argument about my statements, based on publicly ascertainable facts, regarding the present-day Prussian educational administration. There have, however, been two replies in the *Norddeutsche Allgemeine Zeitung* and the manner in which these were done has been so misleading that an official organ of one of the great political parties which, despite the difference in our standpoints, I respect very much, charges me with dredging up events of the remote past in order to attack Prussian ministerial officials of the present day. I would be most reluctant to draw into university questions, on the basis of private information which cannot be verified by anyone else, parliamentarians or political parties which by their nature are inevitably led to interpret such

[34] " Nochmals das ' System Althoff ' ", *Frankfurter Zeitung*, 10 November, 1911.

matters from a political standpoint and for political purposes. I cannot, however, tolerate this accusation, and at the same time I am tired of recurrent misunderstandings. I am, therefore, compelled to state publicly the following points:

(1) Contrary to the denial of the *Norddeutsche Allgemeine Zeitung*, it is still current practice to offer as compensation for the rejection of other appointments, or for other services, implicit promises of prospectively vacant " major " academic posts. This procedure is contrary to the spirit of the university statutes and it is bound to breed " place-hunters ". It must necessarily lead to a system of " sharp practice ", which promotes among the younger academic generation a type of person who feels himself to be a " creature " of the ministerial officials in power at the moment and who, as such, believes he must act accordingly. The practical effect of this policy on the universities on the one side must be the promotion of " practically useful " scientific " nonentities " [35] into academic posts, which according to proper criteria, would go exclusively to persons who are outstanding as scientists and scholars. Its practical influence on the initiation and conduct of research on subjects of practical-political importance must be that these are carried out, not with regard for their practical utility, but rather with an eye to their influence on the prospects of academic advancement.

(2) The ministerial officials sometimes imposed written assurances, acceptances of the obligation of silence—and what is more in a way which expressly equated them with a word of honour—in situations in which the intended and the actual result was an infringement on the custom of taking the expert advice of the faculty. This custom was clearly defined, either legally or conventionally, and corresponded to the enduring interests of the university. The demand for such an obligation of silence must, from the standpoint of the interests of the university, be designated as a demand for an indecent action. The form chosen is incompatible with the customary and proper conduct of official business and cannot be brought into harmony with the position of an official body.

(3) The officials of the educational administration instigated a professor to perform such actions towards his much older colleagues, including some of world-wide reputation, that—as must be known—they have brought him into a conflict of conscience. It also brought down on him the unanimous charge of breach of oath and of immaturity by an arbitration tribunal instituted by colleagues who were not involved and who were, to a man, scholars of world renown; this subjected him to the unanimously and officially expressed censure of his faculty.

As a result of the intrusion of officials into relations between colleagues, academic peace was severely disturbed. Its restoration by peaceful agreement and other collegial means was frustrated. Furthermore, an attempt was made to hinder the activity of the academic arbitration tribunal which was acknowledged by both sides. Finally, the same officials who had been

[35] I wish to state explicitly that I did not apply this expression to Professor Bernhard, whose most essential mistake lay moreover in the fact that he did not recognise the nature of the demands and offers of the educational administration as it was at the time.

involved as one of the contending parties in this dispute presented themselves as judges in it. This whole sequence of action is utterly alien to any dispassionate and honest administration of education. It is no more compatible with the tasks of an official body than it is with the interests and with the foreign and domestic reputation of the universities which are under its authority.

(4) One of the results of the conflict which was caused primarily by the Ministry of Education and which it alone brought to such an acute condition was that a part of the press began a systematic campaign of extremely libellous abuse against highly meritorious scholars of world renown. The officials of the Ministry of Education utilised this part of the press in order to spread certain onesidedly selected facts which they had learnt in connection with their official duties so as to support this crusade. The crusade was bound to injure very grievously the reputation of the universities within Germany and abroad as well. Such conduct cannot be reconciled with the responsibilities of an official body, nor with the sobriety required of a Ministry of Education, nor finally with the most elementary obligations of personal dignity and consideration.

(5) Officials of the Ministry of Education used public funds to publish announcements of lecture courses and seminars in such a way that, by means of the publication or cancellation of these announcements, the private owners of certain periodicals which had no official status could be financially rewarded or damaged, depending not on their official but on their private attitudes towards the personal views of the officials involved. This type of conduct could not but destroy confidence in the sobriety and integrity of the Ministry of Education. It is inconsistent with the best ethical standards of an administrative organ of the state and with the position of a body of officials.

Now, it must—unfortunately—be concluded that the particular officials of the Ministry of Education were of the view that they were permitted to employ the methods just described, that they based this view on the fact that they would not be seriously taken to task by their official superiors for such conduct, and that their official conduct would not be reproved in public. The just assessment of this situation leads necessarily to the conclusion that there is a pattern of conduct in the Ministry of Education which is urgently in need of reform. In view of the public praise which the Minister of Education permitted himself to shower on the mode of administration and on the wide perspective of his bureaucrats and, what is more, the fact that he made his laudation at the expense of the universities, it was high time for university teachers, after their long and angry silence, to issue a protest. They were in agreement in their judgement by an overwhelming majority.

My remarks on these matters have their motives exclusively in considerations of this sort and they serve no political or personal ends. It should also be emphasised again that they do not originate either in the encouragement or in information provided by the university teachers who participated in this protest, nor are they in any way the product of any prior arrangement. I should also add once more—explicitly and finally—that my adduction of examples from the time of Althoff's administration has only been intended to show the continuity of the system. It should also be again emphasised that no derogation of the exceptional accomplishments of this undoubtedly brilliant man and his utterly selfless devotion to his task is implied by the observation that a part of his procedures, and particularly his way of dealing with human beings, is sharply repudiated here.

I have very good grounds for believing that in the future there will be many statements made in public recounting experiences entirely similar to my own in many respects.

This is—I hope—my final word on this matter.

With highest regard,

PROFESSOR MAX WEBER.

XII

A CATHOLIC UNIVERSITY IN SALZBURG [36]

THE press has recently carried a report that a university is to be founded in Salzburg. What is true is that efforts are being made, in association with the theological faculty which exists in Salzburg, to establish a university which will have religious requirements for appointment to some of its secular professorships. This is not only meant in the sense that appointment to certain professorships will be contingent on membership in certain religious bodies. Until recently the survivals from earlier times in certain of the older endowed professorships with similar requirements for appointment could still be found in German universities. Here and there some of them might persist even now. Where such conditions still exist, they are absolutely incompatible with a selection of candidates according to strictly scientific and scholarly criteria. The elimination of these archaic criteria of selection is everywhere in progress. Such requirements do not stipulate that the successful competitor for the appointment must have certain subjective religious convictions.

In Salzburg, however, the imperial nomination of the incumbents of no less than five of the secular professorships is to be dependent on the prior assent of the archbishop. This constitutes a *missio canonica* in every respect. Such a university would naturally not be one likely to be viewed by academic institutions as of equal standing and rights, nor would it indeed be accorded equal privileges. It is said that a Catholic association in Salzburg is providing resources and that the existing German university in Czernovitz is to be transferred there. This would threaten a serious degradation of the latter institution. The plan arises from the commercial interests of local groups in Salzburg. The statement of the interested parties that a ministry of one of the south German states and an imperial German secretary of state were approached, and have been given a promise of acknowledgement of equal standing for the projected institution, scarcely corresponds to the facts. Furthermore,

[36] " Eine katholische Universität in Salzburg ", *Frankfurter Zeitung*, 10 May, 1917.

such an agreement could not help such a religious institution to have its pupils regarded as qualified for degrees in fully-fledged universities or their graduates as qualified to be admitted to habilitation. Extra-academic authorities can do nothing about this.

XIII

THE MEANING OF "ETHICAL NEUTRALITY" IN SOCIOLOGY AND ECONOMICS [37]

IN what follows, when we use the term "evaluation" we will mean, where nothing else is implied or expressly stated, practical value-judgements as to the unsatisfactory or satisfactory character of phenomena subject to our influence. The problem involved in the "freedom" of a given discipline from evaluations of this kind, *i.e.*, the validity and the meaning of this logical principle, is by no means identical with the question which is to be discussed shortly, namely, whether in teaching one should or should not declare one's acceptance of practical evaluations, regardless of whether they are based on ethical principles, cultural ideals or a philosophical outlook. This question cannot be settled scientifically. It is itself entirely a question of practical evaluation, and cannot therefore be definitively resolved. With reference to this issue, a wide variety of views are held, of which we shall only mention the two extremes. At one pole we find (a) the standpoint that there is validity in the distinction between purely logically deducible and purely empirical statements of fact on the one hand, and practical, ethical or philosophical evaluations on the other, but that, nevertheless—or, perhaps, even on that account— both classes of problems properly belong in the university. At the other pole we encounter (b) the proposition that even when the distinction cannot be made in a logically complete manner, it is nevertheless desirable that the assertion of practical evaluations should be avoided as much as possible in teaching.

This second point of view seems to me to be untenable. Particularly untenable is the distinction which is rather often made in our field between evaluations linked with the positions of "political parties" and other sorts of evaluations. This distinction cannot be reasonably made: it obscures the practical implications of the evaluations which are suggested to the audience. Once the assertion of evaluations in university lectures is admitted, the contention that the university teacher should be entirely devoid of "passion" and that he should avoid all subjects which threaten

[37] From "Der Sinn der 'Wertfreiheit' der soziologischen und ökonomischen Wissenschaften", in *Logos*, II (1917), a revised edition of a memorandum written in 1913 for a discussion in the Verein für Sozialpolitik. The essay in *Logos* was reprinted in Weber, Max, *Gesammelte Aufsätze zur Wissenschaftslehre* (Tübingen: J. C. B. Mohr [Paul Siebeck], 1922), pp. 451–461. For the present purpose, I have revised my translation made many years ago and published in Weber, Max, *The Methodology of the Social Sciences* (Glencloe, Illinois: The Free Press, 1949), pp. 1–10. The original memorandum has been published as "Gutachten zur Werturteilsdiskussion im Ausschuss des Vereins zur Sozialpolitik" in Baumgarten, Eduard (ed.), *Max Weber: Werk und Person* (Tübingen: J. C. B. Mohr [Paul Siebeck], 1964), pp. 102–139. [Editor.]

to bring emotion into controversies is a narrow-minded, bureaucratic opinion which every teacher of independent spirit must reject.

Of those scholars who believed that they should not renounce the assertion of practical evaluations in empirical discussions, the most passionate of them—such as Treitschke and, in his own way, Mommsen— were the most tolerable. As a result of their intensely emotional tone, their audiences were enabled to discount the influence of their evaluations in whatever distortion of the facts occurred. Thus, the audiences did for themselves what the lecturers could not do because of their temperaments. The effect on the minds of the students was to produce the same depth of moral feeling which, in my opinion, the proponents of the assertion of practical evaluations in teaching want to assure—but without the audience being confused as to the logical distinctiveness of the different types of propositions. This confusion must of necessity occur whenever both the exposition of empirical facts and the exhortation to espouse a particular evaluative standpoint on important issues are done with the same cool dispassionateness.

The first point of view (a) is acceptable, and can indeed be acceptable from the standpoint of its own proponents, only when the teacher sees it as his unconditional duty—in every single case, even to the point where it involves the danger of making his lecture less stimulating—to make absolutely clear to his audience, and especially to himself, which of his statements are statements of logically deduced or empirically observed facts and which are statements of practical evaluation. Once one has granted the disjunction between the two spheres, it seems to me that doing this is an imperative requirement of intellectual honesty. It is the absolutely minimal requirement in this case.

On the other hand, the question whether one should in general assert practical evaluations in teaching—even with this reservation—is one of practical university policy. On that account, in the last analysis, it must be decided only with reference to those tasks which the individual, according to his own set of values, assigns to the universities. Those who on the basis of their qualifications as university teachers assign to the universities, and thereby to themselves, the universal role of forming character, of inculcating political, ethical, aesthetic, cultural or other beliefs, will take a different position from those who believe it necessary to affirm the proposition and its implications—that university teaching achieves really valuable effects only through specialised training by specially qualified persons. Hence, " intellectual integrity " is the only specific virtue which universities should seek to inculcate. The first point of view can be defended from as many different ultimate evaluative standpoints as the second. The second—which I personally accept—can be derived from a most enthusiastic as well as from a thoroughly modest estimate of the significance of " specialised training ". In order to defend this view, one need not be of the opinion that everyone should become as much a pure " specialist " as possible. One may, on the contrary, espouse it because one does not wish to see the ultimate and deepest personal decisions which a person must make regarding his life, treated exactly as if they were the same as specialised training. One may take this position, however highly one assesses the significance of specialised training, not only for general intellectual training but indirectly also for the self-discipline and the ethical attitude of the young person. Another reason for taking this position is that one does not wish to see the student so influenced by the teacher's suggestions that he is prevented from solving his problems in accordance with the dictates of his own conscience.

Professor von Schmoller's favourable disposition towards the teacher's assertion of his own evaluations in the lecture room is thoroughly intelligible to me personally as the echo of a great epoch which he and his friends helped to create. Even he, however, cannot deny the fact that for the younger generation the objective situation has changed considerably in one important respect. Forty years ago there existed among the scholars working in our discipline, the widespread belief that of the various possible points of view in the domain of practical-political evaluations, ultimately only one was the ethically correct one. (Schmoller himself took this position only to a limited extent.) Today this is no longer the case among the proponents of the assertion of professorial evaluations—as may readily be observed. The legitimacy of the assertion of professorial evaluation is no longer defended in the name of an ethical imperative resting on a relatively simple postulate of justice, which both in its ultimate foundations as well as in its consequences, partly was, and partly seemed to be, relatively unambiguous, and above all relatively impersonal, in consequence of its specifically trans-personal character. Rather, as the result of an inevitable development, it is now done in the name of a motley of "cultural evaluations", *i.e.,* actually subjective cultural demands, or quite openly, in the name of the teachers' alleged "rights of personality". One may well wax indignant over this point of view, but one cannot—because it is a "practical evaluation"—refute it. Of all the types of prophecy, this "personally" tinted type of professorial prophecy is the most repugnant. There is no precedent for a situation in which a large number of officially appointed prophets do their preaching or make their professions of faith, not, as other prophets do, on the streets, or in churches or other public places—or if they do it privately, then in personally chosen sectarian conventicles—but rather regard themselves as best qualified to enunciate their evaluations on ultimate questions "in the name of science" and in the carefully protected quiet of governmentally privileged lecture halls in which they cannot be controlled, or checked by discussion, or subjected to contradiction.

It is an axiom of long standing, which Schmoller on one occasion vigorously espoused, that what takes place in the lecture hall should be entirely confidential and not subject to public discussion. Although it is possible to contend that, even for purely academic purposes, this may occasionally have certain disadvantages, I take the view that a "lecture" should be different from a "speech". The unconfined rigour, matter-of-factness and sobriety of the lecture declines, with definite pedagogical losses, once it becomes the object of publicity through, for example, the press. It is only in the sphere of his specialised qualifications that the university teacher is entitled to this privilege of freedom from outside surveillance or publicity. There is, however, no specialised qualification for personal prophecy, and for this reason it should not be granted the privilege of freedom from contradiction and public scrutiny. Furthermore, there should be no exploitation of the fact that the student, in order to make his way in life, must attend certain educational institutions and take courses with certain teachers with the result that in addition to what he needs—*i.e.*, the stimulation and cultivation of his capacity for understanding and reasoning, and a certain body of factual information—he also gets, slipped in among these, the teacher's own attitude towards the world which even though sometimes interesting is often of no consequence, and which is in any case not open to contradiction and challenge.

Like everyone else, the professor has other opportunities for the propagation of his ideals. When these opportunities are lacking, he can easily create them in an appropriate form, as experience has shown in the case of every honourable attempt. But the professor should not demand the right as a professor to carry the marshal's baton of the statesman or the cultural reformer in his knapsack. This, however, is just what he does when he uses the unassailability of the academic lecture platform for the expression of political—or cultural-political—sentiments. In the press, in public meetings, in associations, in essays, in every avenue which is open to every other citizen, he can and should do what his God or daemon demands. The student should obtain, from his teacher in the lecture hall, the capacity to content himself with the sober execution of a given task; to recognise facts, even those which may be personally uncomfortable, and to distinguish them from his own evaluations. He should also learn to subordinate himself to his task and to repress the impulse to exhibit his personal sensations or other emotional states unnecessarily. This is vastly more important today than it was 40 years ago when the problem did not even exist in its present form. It is not true—as many have insisted—that the " personality " is and should be a " whole ", in the sense that it is distorted when it is not exhibited on every possible occasion.

Every professional task has its own " responsibilities " and should be fulfilled accordingly. In the execution of his professional responsibility, a man should confine himself to it alone and should exclude whatever does not strictly belong to it—particularly his own loves and hates. The powerful personality does not manifest itself by trying to give everything a " personal touch " on every possible occasion. The generation which is now coming of age should, above all, again become used to the thought that " being a personality " is a condition which cannot be intentionally brought about by wanting it and that there is only one way by which it can—perhaps—be achieved: namely, the unreserved devotion to a " task ", whatever it—and its derivative " demands of the hour "—may be in any individual instance. It is in poor taste to mix personal concerns with the specialised analysis of facts. We deprive the word " vocation " of the only significant meaning it still possesses if we fail to adhere to that specific kind of self-restraint which it requires. But whether the fashionable " cult of the personality " seeks to dominate the throne, public office or the professorial chair—its effectiveness is only superficially impressive. Intrinsically, it is very petty and it always has

injurious consequences. It should not be necessary for me to emphasise
that the proponents of the views against which the present essay is
directed can accomplish very little by this sort of cult of the " personality "
for the very reason that it is " personal ". In part, they see the responsibilities of the university teacher in another light, in part they have other
educational ideals which I respect but do not share. For this reason
we must seriously consider not only what they are striving to achieve,
but also how the views which they legitimate by their authority influence
a generation with an already extremely pronounced predisposition to
overestimate its own importance.

Finally, it scarcely needs to be pointed out that many ostensible
opponents of the academic assertion of political evaluations are by no
means justified when they invoke the postulate of " ethical neutrality ",
which they often gravely misunderstand, to discredit cultural and social-
political discussions which take place in public and away from the
university lecture hall. The indubitable existence of this spuriously
" ethically neutral " tendentiousness, which in our discipline is manifested
in the obstinate and deliberate partisanship of powerful interest groups,
explains why a significant number of intellectually honourable scholars
still continue to assert personal preferences in their teaching. They are
too proud to identify themselves with this spurious abstention from
evaluation. I believe that, in spite of this, what in my opinion is right
should be done, and that the influence of the practical evaluations of a
scholar, who confines himself to championing them on appropriate
occasions outside the classroom, will increase when it becomes known
that, inside the classroom, he has the strength of character to do exactly
what he was appointed to do. But these statements are, in their turn, all
matters of evaluation, and hence scientifically undemonstrable.

In any case, the fundamental principle which justifies the practice of
asserting practical evaluations in teaching can be consistently held only
when its proponents demand that the proponents of the evaluations of
all other parties be granted the opportunity to demonstrate the validity
of *their* evaluations from the academic platform.[38] But, in Germany,
insistence on the right of professors to state their preferences has been
associated with the very opposite of the demand for the equal representa-
tion of all tendencies—including the most " extreme ". Schmoller thought
that he was being entirely consistent when he declared that " Marxists
and the Manchester school " were disqualified from holding academic
positions, although he was never so unjust as to ignore their intellectual
accomplishments. It is exactly on these points that I could never agree
with our honoured master. One obviously ought not in one breath to
justify the expression of evaluations in teaching—and when the conclu-
sions are drawn therefrom, point out that the university is a state

[38] Hence we cannot be satisfied with the Dutch principle of emancipation of even
theological faculties from confessional requirements, together with the freedom to found
universities as long as the following conditions are observed: guarantee of finances, main-
tenance of standards as to qualifications of teachers, and the right of private endowment
of professorships coupled with the founder's right to present an incumbent for the chair.
This gives the advantage to those with large sums of money and to groups which are
already in power. Only clerical circles have, as far as we know, made use of this privilege.

institution for the training of "loyal" civil servants. Such a procedure makes the university, not into a specialised technical school—which appears to be so degrading to many teachers—but rather into a theological seminary, although it does not have the religious dignity of the latter.

Attempts have been made to set certain purely "logical" limits to the range of evaluations which should be allowed in university teaching. One of our foremost professors of law once explained, in discussing his opposition to the exclusion of socialists from university posts, that he too would be unwilling to accept an "anarchist" as a teacher of law since anarchists, in principle, deny the validity of law—and he regarded this argument as conclusive. My own opinion is exactly the opposite. An anarchist can surely be a good legal scholar. And if he is such, then indeed the Archimedean point of his convictions, which is outside the conventions and presuppositions which are so self-evident to us, could enable him to perceive problems in the fundamental postulates of legal theory which escape those who take them for granted. The most fundamental doubt is one source of knowledge. The jurist is no more responsible for "proving" the value of these cultural objects which are bound up with "law", than the physician is responsible for demonstrating that the prolongation of life should be striven for under all conditions. Neither of them can do this with the means at their disposal. If, however, one wishes to turn the university into a forum for discussion of practical evaluations, then it obviously is obligatory to permit the most unrestricted freedom of discussion of fundamental questions from all standpoints.

Is this feasible? Today the most decisive and important political evaluations are denied expression in German universities by the very nature of the present political situation. For all those to whom the interests of the national society transcend any of its individual concrete institutions, it is a question of central importance whether the conception which prevails today regarding the position of the monarch in Germany is reconcilable with the world interests of the country, and with the means—war and diplomacy—through which these are pursued. It is not always the worst patriots nor even anti-monarchists who give a negative answer to this question, and who doubt the possibility of lasting success in both these spheres unless some profound changes are made. Everyone knows, however, that these vital questions of our national life cannot be discussed with full freedom in German universities.[39] In view of the fact that certain evaluations which are of decisive political significance are permanently prohibited in university discussion, it seems to me to be only in accord with the dignity of a representative of science and scholarship to be silent about such evaluations as he is allowed to expound.

In no case, however, should the unresolvable question—unresolvable because it is ultimately a question of evaluations—as to whether one may, must, or should champion certain practical evaluations in teaching, be confused with the purely *logical* discussion of the relationship of evalua-

[39] This is by no means peculiar to Germany. In almost every country there exist, openly or hidden, actual restraints. The only differences are in the particular evaluative positions which are thus excluded.

tions to empirical disciplines such as sociology and economics. Any confusion on this point will hamper the thoroughness of the discussion of the logical problem. However, even the solution of the logical problem will provide no aid in seeking to answer the other question, beyond the two purely logically required conditions of clarity and an explicit distinction by the teacher of the different classes of problems.

Nor need I discuss further whether the distinction between empirical propositions or statements of fact and practical evaluations is " difficult " to make. It is. All of us, those of us who take this position as well as others, come up against it time and again. But as the exponents of the so-called " ethical economics ", particularly, should be aware, even though the moral law is unfulfillable, it is nonetheless " imposed " as a duty. Self-scrutiny would perhaps show that the fulfilment of this postulate is especially difficult, just because we reluctantly refuse to approach the very alluring subject of evaluation with a titillating " personal touch ". Every teacher has observed that the faces of his students light up and they become more interested when he begins to make a profession of faith, and that the attendance at his lectures is greatly increased by the expectation that he will do so. Everyone knows furthermore that, in the competition for students, universities when making recommendations for promotion, will often give a prophet, however minor, who can fill the lecture halls, the upper hand over a much weightier and more sober scholar who does not offer his own evaluations. Of course, it is understood that the prophet will leave untouched the politically dominant or conventional evaluations which are generally accepted at the time. Only the spuriously " ethically-neutral " prophet who speaks for powerful groups has, of course, better opportunities for promotion as a result of the influence which these groups have on the prevailing political powers.

I regard all this as very unsatisfactory, and I will therefore not go into the proposition that the demand for abstention from evaluation is " petty " and that it makes lectures " boring ". I will not go into the question as to whether lecturers on specialised empirical problems must seek above all to be " interesting ". For my own part, in any case, I fear that a lecturer who makes his lectures stimulating by the intrusion of personal evaluations will, in the long run, weaken the students' taste for sober empirical analysis.

I will acknowledge without further discussion that it is possible, under the guise of eliminating all practical evaluations, to insinuate such evaluations with especial force by simply " letting the facts speak for themselves ". The better kind of parliamentary and electoral speeches in Germany operate in this way—and quite legitimately, given their purposes. No words should be wasted in declaring that all such procedures in university lectures, particularly if one is concerned with the observance of this separation, are, of all abuses, the most abhorrent. The fact, however, that a dishonestly created illusion of the fulfilment of an ethical imperative can be passed off as the reality, constitutes no criticism of the imperative itself. At any rate, even if the teacher does not believe that he should deny himself the right of rendering evaluations, he should

make it absolutely *explicit* to the students and to himself that he is
doing so.

Finally, we must oppose to the utmost the widespread view that scientific " objectivity " is achieved by weighing the various evaluations against
one another and making a " statesman-like " compromise among them.
The " middle way " is not only just as undemonstrable scientifically—
with the means of the empirical sciences—as the " most extreme "
evaluations: in the sphere of evaluations, it is the least unequivocal. It
does not belong in the university—but rather in political programmes,
government offices, and in parliament. The sciences, both normative and
empirical, are capable of rendering an inestimable service to persons
engaged in political activity by telling them that (1) these and these
" ultimate " evaluative positions are conceivable with reference to this
practical problem; and (2) that such and such are the facts which you
must take into account in making your choice between these evaluative
positions. And with this we come to the real problem.

<h1 style="text-align:center">XIV</h1>

<h2 style="text-align:center">SCIENCE AS A VOCATION [40]</h2>

I AM to speak, according to your wish, on " science as a vocation ". Now,
we economists have a certain pedantic custom, to which I shall adhere,
of always beginning with the objective situation. Hence, in this case,
I will start with the question: What are the material features of the
cultivation of science and scholarship as a vocation? Today this is
equivalent to asking: What is the position of a graduate who is resolved
to enter upon a scientific or scholarly career in the academic world? In
order to understand the distinctiveness of the German situation, it is
useful to proceed comparatively and to picture to ourselves how the
matter stands in the United States, where the divergence from Germany
in this respect is greatest.

In Germany the career of a young man who finds his vocation in
science begins normally as a *Privatdozent*. He " habilitates " at a university after consultation with and with the consent of the representatives
of his special discipline, already having submitted a book and undergone
a largely perfunctory examination in the presence of the faculty. Paid not
with a regular salary, but only by the capitation fees of the students who
attend his courses, he lectures on subjects which he himself chooses within
the terms of his *venia legenda*.

In America, an academic career usually begins in quite another fashion,
namely, by appointment as an " assistant ". This is somewhat similar
to the practice in Germany where, in the large institutes of natural
science research and in the medical faculties, formal " habilitation " as
a *Privatdozent* is achieved only by a fraction of the assistants, and even
in those cases, only after the lapse of some time. In practice, this means
that in Germany the career of a scientist or scholar depends on his
having private means, for it is extremely hazardous for a young scholar,

[40] *Wissenschaft als Beruf* (Munich and Leipzig: Duncker und Humblot, 1919), pp. 3–15.

who has no financial resources of his own, to expose himself to the conditions of an academic career. He must be able to carry on like this for at least some years without in any way knowing whether, at the end of this unstipulated period, he will have the opportunity to obtain an appointment which will enable him to support himself. In the United States, on the contrary, there is a bureaucratic system in which the young man is paid from the very beginning—although moderately to be sure. Usually his salary barely corresponds to the wages of a not entirely unskilled labourer. Nevertheless, he begins with an apparently secure position, for he receives a definite salary. The rule is that like the German assistant, he may be dismissed, and he has to be ready for it should he fall short of expectations. However, this threat disappears if he " packs the house ". This threat of dismissal does not exist for the German *Privatdozent*. Once he is appointed, he remains permanently. It is, of course, true that he has no " claims " to advancement. Yet, he has the understandable idea that if he has been a *Privatdozent* for some years, he has a kind of moral right to consideration; he may even think this when the habilitation of other *Privatdozenten* is in question.

Whether one should systematically habilitate every scholar who has given evidence of fitness, or whether one should take " teaching needs " into consideration, *i.e.*, whether one should confer a monopoly on the already habilitated *Privatdozenten*, is a difficult dilemma which is connected with the dual character of the academic vocation shortly to be mentioned. The decision has, for the most part, been rendered in favour of the second alternative. This increases the danger that the full professor in the particular field, even if he is most conscientious, will favour his own students. Personally, I have followed the principle that a scholar who has taken his degree under me must demonstrate his worth elsewhere and habilitate at another university under some other professor. But, as a result, one of my best students was rejected at another place because no one believed that this was the real reason for his attempt to habilitate there.

A further difference between Germany and America is that in Germany the *Privatdozent* generally has less to do with teaching than he would like. He has, it is true, the formal right to teach any subject in his field. The actual exercise of this right, however, is considered an unfair lack of consideration towards the older *Privatdozenten*, and as a rule the " main " courses are given by the full professors while the *Privatdozent* occupies himself with the auxiliary courses. The advantage is that his early years, even though he does not intend it that way, are free for scientific work.

In America things are organised on a different principle. It is indeed in his earlier years that the assistant is heavily overburdened, precisely because he is *paid*. In a German department, for instance, a full professor will give a three-hour course on Goethe and that is all—while the younger assistant is lucky if his assignment of 12 hours per week includes, besides the hack-work of teaching German grammar, an opportunity to lecture on poets of about the rank of Uhland. The curriculum is prescribed by the authority of the department; the assistant is just as dependent in this respect as the institute assistant in Germany.

Now it is quite clear that, in Germany, most recent developments in our universities in the various fields of science and scholarship are moving in the same direction as in the United States. Large research institutes in medicine or the natural sciences are " state capitalistic " enterprises. They cannot be administered without plant, equipment and other resources on a large scale, and the results there are the same as they are wherever the capitalistic type of organisation—*i.e.,* the " separation of the worker from the means of production "—is established. The worker —in this case, the assistant—must use the means of production which are made available by the state. He is, in consequence, just as dependent on the director of the institute as the clerk in a factory is on the manager, since the director of the institute believes quite sincerely that the institute is " his " institute and that he is master there. The German scientific assistant, accordingly, frequently leads the same kind of precarious existence as anyone in a quasi-proletarian occupation and as the assistant in the American university.

Like German life in general, German academic life is becoming Americanised in very important respects. This trend, I am convinced, will continue in those fields where, as is still largely the case today in my own field, the scholar himself owns the means of production—essentially, his library—just as the craftsmen did in the past. This development is now in full swing.

The technical advantages, similar to those of all capitalistic, bureaucratised organisations, are certainly indisputable. But the " spirit " which prevails in them is different from the traditional atmosphere once characteristic of the German universities. There is an extraordinarily wide gulf, in overt behavior and in attitude, between the head of such a large capitalistic academic enterprise and the old-style full professor. But I do not wish to elaborate this here. Internally, just as externally, the traditional university constitution has become a fiction. One essential feature of the academic career has, however, remained and has even become more pronounced: it is still simply a matter of accident whether a *Privatdozent* or an assistant ever suceeds in becoming a professor or an institute director. Accident is not only common—it is extraordinarily frequent. I know of scarcely any career in the world in which it plays such a role. I am perhaps all the more entitled to say so, since I, personally, am indebted to several absolutely accidental factors for the fact that, while I was still very young, I became a full professor in a field in which at that time my contemporaries had undoubtedly accomplished more than I had. I flatter myself by believing that I have, on the basis of this experience, a somewhat sharpened eye for the undeserved fate of many with whom chance has played just the opposite role and who, despite all their excellence, have not achieved the position to which they were entitled.

Now the fact that chance, and not ability as such, plays such a large part, does not depend alone or even primarily on those failings which naturally are just as operative in this type of selection as in any other. It would be unjust to blame the personal inadequacies of faculties or officials in ministries of education for the fact that so many mediocrities play such a prominent role in the universities. Rather, this is an inevitable consequence of human interaction, particularly interaction between organisations and, in this case, interaction between the faculty which recommends an appointment and the ministry of education. A counterpart to this can be traced through many centuries in the papal elections which represent the most important example of a similar type of selection. Only rarely does the cardinal who is said to be the " favourite " come out on top. As a rule, it is the candidate in the second or third position. The same is true of the presidential nominations in the party conventions in the United States. Only exceptionally does the original favourite win the " nomination " at the party convention and enter the election. Instead, it is usually the second- and often the third-ranking candidate.

American sociologists already have a technical terminology to refer to these kinds of events, and it would be quite interesting to investigate the process of selection in situations in which consensus is required. We will not do this today. These laws of selection apply to academic bodies as well and we should not wonder that mistakes occur quite often. What is really remarkable is that despite everything the number of correct appointments is, relatively speaking, so considerable. Acquiescent mediocrities or climbers have the odds in their favour in matters of academic appointment or promotion only where, as in certain states, parliament—or as in Germany hitherto, the monarch—both operate in the same way, and as now, revolutionary dictators, intervene for *political* reasons.

No university teacher likes to think about discussions regarding appointments, for they are rarely pleasant. And nonetheless I must say that goodwill, the desire to decide exclusively on grounds relevant to the subject, has always, without exception, been present in the many cases which have come to my attention.

For it should be emphatically asserted that it is not because of the defects of decisions requiring consensus that the determination of academic destinies is so much a matter of accident. Every young man, who believes he is called to an academic career, must make clear to himself that the task which awaits him has two faces. He should be qualified not only as a research worker but also as a teacher. The two are neither identical nor inseparable. One can be very outstanding in research and atrocious as a teacher; to illustrate this contention, I will cite only the teaching practice of such men as Helmholtz or Ranke. Nor are they rare exceptions.

The situation is such that our universities—especially the small ones—are engaged in the most ludicrous sort of competition with one another for students. The lodging-house proprietors of the university towns greet the thousandth student with a celebration, the two thousandth preferably with a torch procession. Lecture fees in one department—it should be openly admitted—are affected by an appointment with " drawing power " in the neighbouring department; even disregarding this, attendance at lectures is quantitatively tangible evidence whereas high quality in research is imponderable and is often, and quite naturally in the case of bold innovators, controversial. Almost everything is thought of in terms of the prospect of the immeasurable blessing and value of a large audience. If it said of a *Privatdozent* that he is a poor teacher, it amounts almost to an academic death sentence, even though he be one of the foremost scholars in his field. The question, however, as to whether he is a good or poor teacher is answered by the attendance with which the students honour him.

The fact that students flock to a teacher is, however, determined in unbelievably large measure by purely superficial factors such as temperament and even tone of voice. After quite extensive experience and sober consideration, I am very suspicious of large audiences, however unavoidable they may be. Democracy should be practised where it is appropriate. Scientific training, however, if we are to carry it on in accord with the traditions of the German universities, implies the existence of a certain type of intellectual aristocracy. We should not conceal this fact from ourselves. Perhaps the most difficult of all pedagogical tasks is the exposition of scientific or scholarly problems in such a manner that an untrained but receptive mind can understand them and think independently about them. This last point is the decisive one for us. But whether it is well done or not cannot be decided by the size of a lecture audience. And—to return once more to our theme—even this skill is a highly personal gift and it is not by any means necessarily associated with the qualities of a scientific or scholarly investigator. In contrast with France, Germany has no body of the " immortals " of science and scholarship. German university traditions require on the contrary that we do justice both to research and to teaching. The coexistence of these two talents in the same person is, however, wholly a matter of chance.

Academic careers are then sorely beset by chance. When a young scientist or scholar comes to seek advice about habilitation, the responsibility which one assumes in advising him is heavy indeed. If he is a Jew, one naturally tells him: *lasciate ogni speranza*. But the others, too, must be asked with the utmost seriousness: " Do you think that, year after year, you will be able to stand seeing one mediocrity after another promoted over you, and still not become embittered and dejected? " Of course, the answer is always: " Naturally, I live only for my ' calling '." But only in a very few cases have I found them able to undergo it without suffering spiritual damage.

These things have to be said about the external conditions of the academic career.

I think however that you really wish to hear about something else, about the inner or deeper vocation of science. In these days, the innermost core, in the face of the objective organisation of science as a vocation, is affected by the fact that science has entered into a stage of specialisation such as has hitherto been unknown and from which it will never re-emerge. The individual can be sure of accomplishing something really definitive and complete in the field of science, only if he follows the lines required by the most rigorous specialisation. Every investigator who invades neighbouring fields, as we occasionally do, and as indeed the sociologist, for example, must repeatedly do, is oppressed by the resigned feeling that he is merely providing the specialist with useful hypotheses which the latter, from his specialised standpoint, would not easily come upon; the invader is left with the feeling that his own work must inevitably remain far from complete and imperfect. Only through rigorous specialisation does the scientific worker gain the possibility, once and perhaps never again, of feeling a sense of definitive achievement—the feeling that he had accomplished something which will really endure. A really definitive and outstanding achievement is always a specialised achievement. Whoever lacks the ability to put blinders on himself, so to speak, and to convince himself that the fate of his soul depends on whether his particular interpretation of a certain passage in a manuscript is correct, will always be alien to science and scholarship. He will never be able to " experience " a sense of what is involved in scientific work. Without this rare intoxication, ridiculed by those on the outside, without this passion, this feeling that " thousands of years must pass before you enter into life and thousands more wait in silence "—depending on whether your interpretation was correct, science is not your vocation and you should do something else. For nothing is worth-while for a human being as a human being which he cannot do with passionate devotion.

The fact remains however that passionate devotion alone, regardless of how intense it is, and of how unqualified it is by other considerations, does not produce scientific results of the highest quality. It is, to be sure, a prerequisite of the " inspiration " which is decisive. Today, in certain circles of the younger generation, there is a very widespread notion that science has become a problem in arithmetic which is carried on in laboratories or statistical bureaus, not by the " whole person " but by cool, calculating reason " as if it were something produced in a factory ". Such ideas reveal not even the slightest understanding of what takes place either in a factory or in a laboratory. In the former as well as in the latter, a person must have an " inspiration " and " idea ", if he is to accomplish something valuable. This " inspiration " cannot be forced. It has nothing to do with dispassionate calculation. It is of course true that the latter is also an indispensable prerequisite for intellectual accomplishment. No sociologist, for example, should regard himself even in his old age as above spending many months doing tens of thousands of quite trivial computations. One cannot with impunity leave everything to mechanical devices if one wishes to produce something significant— and what is finally produced is often wretchedly little. But if he does not have some " idea " to guide his computations or, in the course of the computation, about the scope of his emerging results, then even this pittance will not be produced. This " idea " usually arises only in the course of quite hard work. But not always, to be sure.

The hunch of a dilettante about a certain phenomenon may have the same or greater significance than a specialist's. We owe many of our very best hypotheses and insights to dilettantes. The dilettante is distinguished from the specialist—as Helmholtz said about Robert Mayer—only by his lack of a definite procedure, and consequently by his inability to control and to assess or to realise and exploit the potentialities of his hunch. An imaginative idea is no substitute for work. On the other hand, work is no substitute for imaginative insight; diligent work, no more than passionate devotion, is capable of compelling insight. Both—particularly, both together—draw it out. But it comes only when it pleases and it does not consult our desires. It is in fact correct that the best ideas come, as Ihering once said, while smoking a cigar at one's ease, or as Helmholtz, with scientific exactitude, reports of himself, during a walk on a gradually ascending street, or in some similar way; in any case, they come when one does not expect them—and not when one is puzzling and pondering at one's desk. These ideas, however, would not have arisen in the imagination had they not been preceded by pondering at the desk and by incessant questioning. At any rate, the scientist and scholar must reckon with the chance which attends every piece of research—the chance that inspiration might or might not come. One can be a very good research worker and still never have had a single valuable idea of one's own.

It is, however, a serious mistake to believe that this occurs only in science and that, for example, the situation in a commercial office differs from that in a laboratory. A merchant or a large-scale industrialist without "business imagination", *i.e.*, without ideas, brilliant original ideas, remains at best a clerk or a technician; he will never be able to create a new organisation. The role inspiration plays is no greater in the field of science—as academic conceit would have us believe—than it is in the mastery of practical problems by a modern entrepreneur. On the other hand, it plays no less a role in science than it does in the field of art; this point is often disregarded. It is childish to believe that a mathematician at his desk could arrive at some scientifically important result with only a slide rule or other mechanical instrument or calculating machine; the mathematical imagination of a Weierstrass is naturally differently oriented, both in intention and results, from the imagination of an artist, and it is, qualitatively, fundamentally different. But psychologically they are the same—both are distinguished by a sort of intoxication (in the sense of Plato's "mania") and "inspiration".

Whether one is scientifically inspired depends on factors of which we know little aside from the fact that they involve "talent". It is not, however, because of an acceptance of this indubitable truth that an intense enthusiasm for certain new idols has become so prevalent among the younger generation—although that prevalence is quite understandable. The idols of "personality" and "experience"—understood as a state of mind—are now worshipped at every street corner and in every periodical. They are closely related to each other: there is a widespread view that "experience" nourishes "personality" and belongs to it. There is a great deal of worry about "experiencing"—since this is necessary to the mode of life proper to a person laying claim to "personality". If one has not undergone "experience" then, according to this doctrine, one must at least act as if one actually does possess this gift of grace. Previously this "experience" used to be called "sensitivity", and there used to be, I believe, a more adequate conception of what constituted "personality".

In science, only the person who serves his task has "personality". And this is true not only of science. We know of no great artist who would have done otherwise than serve his task, and only it. Even with a personality of the order of Goethe's, the fact that he took the liberty of making his life into a work of art had its revenge on his artistic achievement. This might seem doubtful, but one must be a Goethe even to dare to allow oneself this privilege. It must, at least, be admitted that, even with a person of the order of Goethe such as appears once in a thousand years, this privilege does not go unpaid for. In politics the situation is exactly the same, but we will say nothing of it today. In science, however, he is certainly no " personality " who, as an impressario of the subject to which he should devote himself, appears on the stage seeking to legitimate himself through " experience " and asks: " How can I show that I am something more than a ' specialist '? How can I manage to say something —either in the form or in the substance of my work—in a way in which no one has ever said it before? " Today this is a very widespread phenomenon and it has a debasing effect. Instead of being elevated, by devotion to their tasks, to the dignity of the subject which they purport to serve, those who hold such views degrade themselves. The situation is no different among artists.

Unlike these necessary conditions which are common to both science and art, there is one fundamental feature which distinguishes them rather sharply from one another. Scientific work postulates the progress of knowledge. In art, on the contrary, there is—in this sense—no progress. A work of art of a period which has elaborated new technical devices such as, for instance, the principles of perspective, is not, on that account, necessarily superior aesthetically to a work of art produced without any knowledge of those devices and principles—as long as it is appropriate to its content and form, *i.e.*, as long as it has chosen and formed its object in a manner which is artistically appropriate to the absence of those conditions and procedures. A work of art is really a " fulfilment " in an artistic sense and is never rendered obsolete by a subsequent work of art. Individuals may estimate its significance for themselves differently, but none can ever say of a work which is a " fulfilment " in the artistic sense that it has been " surpassed " by another one which is likewise a " fulfilment ". In contrast with this, every scientist knows that what he achieves will be outdated in 10, 20 or 50 years. Every scientific " fulfilment " raises new " problems " and should be " surpassed " and rendered obsolete. This is the fate—and indeed the significance of work in science, to this it is subordinated and devoted. This distinguishes it from all the other spheres of culture which also demand submission and devotion.

Everyone who wishes to serve science must accommodate himself to this. Scientific achievements can, it is true, endure as " satisfactions " on account of their artistic quality; they can also remain important as a means of training for actual scientific work. But—it should be repeated— it is not only our fate, but also our goal that we should be scientifically transcended. We cannot work without the hope that others will go further than we have. In principle, this progress goes on *ad infinitum*.

And, with this, we come to the problem of the meaning of science. For it is not self-evident that an activity, governed by such a law, should be intrinsically meaningful and reasonable. Why do we carry on an activity which can never be completed? We can answer that we do it first of all

for purely practical, technological purposes in the wider sense, *i.e.*, so as to
be able to guide our practical conduct in accordance with the expectations
which scientific analysis makes available to us. Good! But this means
something only to the man of action. What, however, is the attitude of
the scientist and scholar himself towards his calling—if he seeks to
discover its deeper meaning? He maintains that he pursues science " for
its own sake ", and not only so that others should be able to achieve
business or technical success, to be better nourished, to dress better, to
have better lighting and to govern better. But what does he believe he is
meaningfully accomplishing with these creations which are always doomed
to become obsolete—what is his purpose in allowing himself to be bound
within this specialised enterprise which runs on into infinity? This
requires a few general remarks.